SURFING THE MENU
again

SURFING THE MENU *again*

With more than eighty exciting fresh-food recipes

Ben O'Donoghue AND Curtis Stone

Photographs by Steve Brown, Craig Kinder and Ewan Robinson

ABC
Books

The publishers would like to thank the following organisations for kindly supplying homewares and props for use during the full-page food photography: Alex Liddy (pp. 32, 72, 107, 134, 182, 188, 200), Bison Homewares (pp.17, 84, 108, 148, 163, 177), Bodum (p. 126, 133, 145, 181, 199, 210), The Ceramic Shed (pp. 25, 42, 126, 137, 163), Dandi (p. 199), David Edmonds (p. 177), Design Mode International (pp. 17, 22, 72, 95, 134, 148), Jarass (p. 21, 49, 151, 158, 178, 181, 182, 200) and Sheldon & Hammond (p. 83).

Published by ABC Books for the
AUSTRALIAN BROADCASTING CORPORATION
GPO Box 9994 Sydney NSW 2001

National Library of Australia
Cataloguing-in-Publication entry
    O'Donoghue, Ben.
    Surfing the menu again: with over 80 exciting fresh food
    recipes.
    Includes index.
    ISBN 10: 07333 1496 1
    ISBN 13: 978 0733 1496 4
    1. Cookery, Australian. I. Stone, Curtis. II. Brown,
    Steve. III. Robinson, Ewan. IV. Kinder, Craig. V.
    Australian Broadcasting Corporation. VI. Title.
641.5994

Designed by Nada Backovic
Copyedited by Megan Johnston
Food styling by Michelle Noerianto
Home economists Rebecca Truda, Tracy Rutherford,
    Christine Sheppard and Julie Ballard
Typeset by Kirby Jones and Nada Backovic
Jacket design by Nada Backovic
Jacket photography by Craig Kinder and Steve Brown
Set in Univers 10/16pt
Colour reproduction by Pageset, Victoria
Printed and bound in Singapore by Tien Wah Press

5 4 3 2

Contents

BEN O'DONOGHUE

Even though I was born in England and have spent almost eight years there working, I think of myself as an Australian and can't wait to get back to visit friends and family and to share great food and wine with them.

I almost fell into working as a chef. I'd planned to finish school and train to be a teacher, but in the summer holidays between school and college I found myself working on Western Australia's Rottnest Island, in the Rottnest Restaurant. It was as if I suddenly knew what I wanted to do with my life. So I became apprenticed and worked at a couple of seafood restaurants before heading to Sydney.

There I worked as sous chef at Goodfellas, a very hot new restaurant in Newtown. In 1993 it was awarded Best New Restaurant in *The Sydney Morning Herald Good Food Guide*.

In 1996, I decided to try my luck in the UK, where I was pretty lucky to immediately get a job at The River Café, which, of course, is where I met Jamie Oliver and went on to work on some episodes of his early series and cookbooks.

I moved on to Monte's, a private restaurant and bar in Knightsbridge where I was head chef for three years. I had started to do some television work, which led to *The Best* for the BBC in 2002; it became a success and led to a book of the series.

Then another television opportunity came my way: the first series of *Surfing the Menu* and the book that went with that. Everything always happens at once, so at about the same time I leapt at the challenge of taking control of The Atlantic Bar and Grill in Piccadilly, *and* my daughter Ruby was born.

Dee and I decided to get married – in Australia, of course, because our families and so many friends are there. And, as things always happen at once, the very persistent producer of *Surfing the Menu* wore me down and got me to agree to do series 2 while I was here. So we did get married (and Ruby was the most fantastic flower girl you ever did see) but somehow I ended up giving up my honeymoon to film two episodes of the show. They're a bit like that, producers.

But, in the end, who could turn down the opportunity to have a great time with old mates from the first series, or resist all that simply superb fresh produce and those brilliant flavour combinations we discovered travelling around the country? Not me.

Ben O'Donoghue

Curtis Stone

CURTIS STONE

Over the past few years my life taken many new turns. It started when a publisher walked through the doors of Quo Vadis, the restaurant where I had been head chef for two years and one of a number of very successful establishments owned by Marco Pierre White. The book the publisher had come to speak to me about was called *London On A Plate*, which was to feature twenty of London's best restaurants and their chefs.

Of course I agreed to be a part of it! And when the finished book was sent to me, not only did it say on the front cover 'Recipes from London's Finest Chefs', but I was in the company of the likes of John Burton Race and Paul Gayler, two chefs I admired greatly. I was blown away at the time, but I had no idea what being in the book was about to mean for my future career.

What came next was an agent, magazine articles, regular television appearances in the UK and a load of cooking demos all over the country. Along with this came long waiting lists at the restaurant – and I suddenly appreciated the power of the media.

I was offered the first series of 'Surfing the Menu' and, as I've always said that for a chef to produce good food he or she needs to be at the restaurant cooking every night, I resigned from Quo Vadis to come back to Australia. What an experience filming that series was! And working on the book that went with it.

Afterwards I went back to London and accepted a job at The Blue Bird Club. I was there for six months, setting up a kitchen and rewriting the brasserie menu with Neil Haydock (the chef of the Brassiere). I enjoyed my time working for Sir Terence Conran; he was a big inspiration with his twin loves of food and design.

My next move was back to Australia to host the monster reality television show 'My Restaurant Rules', quickly followed by the filming the second series of 'Surfing the Menu' and working on this companion book.

In the past year I have enjoyed myself a lot. But there has been one thing missing in my life: the buzz, excitement and sheer madness of a service in a busy restaurant. That's the reason I am heading back to London to find my next restaurant, so I can cook all day in a busy kitchen.

In life you are very lucky if you find the one thing that you have a real passion for. And I think that I am the luckiest man in the world. There is nothing on this earth that makes me happier than cooking something perfectly and then watching the expression on someone's face when they eat it.

Albany

Albany

Fruits of the harvest from near and far

Albany is on the southern coast of Western Australia. It was the first official settlement in Western Australia, originally chosen because of its beautiful natural harbour — and because the French were known to be interested the region too. On one French expedition alone, that of Nicolas Baudin, more than 240 Australian landmarks were discovered and given French names, plus they collected samples of 2542 new animal species and took back over 180,000 specimens. Many bays and features near Albany still have French names like Two People's Bay (Baie des Deux Peuples), Point D'Entrecasteaux and the obvious Frenchman's Bay.

A little further around the coast are further examples like Recherche Archipelago, Hamlin Bay, Cape Freycinet, Cape Mentelle, Cape Clairault and Cape Naturaliste. Sadly for Baudin, he never made it back to France with his discoveries; he died of tuberculosis in Mauritius on the voyage home.

Albany is also a port that services the rich fishing grounds to the south and the farmlands that spread north for hundreds of kilometres.

Lamb always reminds us of Sunday lunches back here in Oz with our families. It's our ultimate comfort food. Roast veggies, gravy — yum. So our first stop on this journey was to visit local farmer, Charlie Hicks. Charlie's claim to fame, apart from the fact that his wife Margaret makes a mean coconut and chocolate brownie, is that he is breeding and selling lamb new to Australia, that he calls Lambouillet.

Lambouillet is a Rambouillet lamb (originating from Rambouillet, a village outside Paris, France), which Charlie has successfully cross-bred back to the merino variety. What you end up with is a hardy sheep with meat lighter in colour, texture and flavour, perhaps as veal is to beef.

Charlie's advice was simple: don't overcook the lamb. Now there's a man after our own hearts. We reckon overcooking lamb comes from Australia's British connection, whereas the Mediterraneans know how to treat lamb: simply cooked, pink on the inside.

Then there's Ray Gerovich, he loves pigs. But that doesn't mean, when it's time, he doesn't send this little piggy off to market.

Ray decided that there must be a better way than just to put pigs into a huge piggery, locked in small cells. In the northern hemisphere there is an argument to be made for such methods because of lack of space, and also the fact that in winter snows can be metres deep. But here in Albany and other parts of Australia, where there's plenty of room and a year-round mild climate, those arguments go out the window.

During the day, Ray's pigs wander around in the paddocks. They dig it up. They wallow in it. They have fun. And each evening they come running back to the barn knowing there's a feed of grain waiting for them, and that's after eating all day in the field. Maybe that's why they're called pigs!

Now, 'Oranje Tractor' has got to be one of the weirdest names for a vineyard and winery we've ever seen. But the orange tractor that greeted us and does a lot of the hard work around the farm was a bit of a clue.

Down in that mild area, cool climate grapes flourish. Among them rieslings, semillon-sauvignon blanc and pinot noirs. And at Oranje Tractor they make some very nice wines — and they've won some very nice awards with them, too.

Pam Lincoln and Murray Gomme have made this vineyard organic for one simple reason: it just feels right. Rather than fight against nature, they'd rather work with it. Which is why the guinea fowl and chickens run loose in the vineyard, eating all the bugs.

They also have some amazing vegetables and fruit growing such as chocolate capsicum, tangerines and strawberry guavas — many come from Herronswood, the heirloom plant specialists that we were to visit on the Mornington Peninsula!

Who would have thought that driving through typical Australian countryside you'd come across a working Dutch windmill based on a perfectly proportioned sixteenth-century design?

This windmill, The Lilly, was a labour of love for Pluen Hitzert, who moved with his family to Australia in 1980, and who took eight years to research the design and another seven years to actually build it himself. The windmill turns a full 360 degrees, is rigged like a ship (as were the originals), and features beams from the old Albany jetty, too.

Windmills like this were quite commonplace in Australia's early days; there were about eighty in total and some thirty-six in Sydney Town alone. Today, however, there isn't one like it in all of Australia. The Lilly still works, too, grinding wholemeal flour every day from the grain that is grown on the property.

Rebuilding must be in the Hitzerts' blood because they also disassembled, transported and rebuilt the old Gnowangerup Railway Station on their property, and now use it as a restaurant.

Freshly shucked oysters with avocado and chilli cream

For variation on the standard oyster with lemon juice, make up a small pot of this lovely, silky, citrus-fresh avocado cream.

SERVES 4

24 oysters, freshly shucked
2 avocados, halved
1 large red chilli, chopped
2 tablespoons lime juice
60 g/2¼ oz crème fraîche
sea salt and freshly ground black pepper

1. Arrange the oysters on a platter so that they are sitting level.

2. Place the avocado, chilli and lime juice in a food processor and process until smooth. Pass through a fine sieve. Stir through the crème fraîche and season with the salt and pepper.

3. Serve the avocado and chilli cream in individual pots with spoons so that people can place spoonfuls on top of the oysters. Freshly ground black pepper can be added to taste.

Curtis Stone

Roasted artichokes with quinoa and seed salad

There are so many ways to cook artichokes, but this is one of my favourites. It's so easy and quick. Combined with the salad it really is a vegetarian sensation.

SERVES 4

8 long stem artichokes
lemon juice, to taste
2–3 tablespoons olive oil
sea salt and freshly ground black pepper
8 sprigs of thyme

Salad
$^1/_2$ cup quinoa*
1 garlic clove
$^1/_4$ bunch of basil, leaves picked
1 tablespoon lemon juice
1 tablespoon olive oil
$^1/_4$ cup linseeds
$^1/_4$ cup pumpkin seeds
$^1/_4$ cup sunflower seeds
$^1/_4$ cup pine nuts
sea salt and freshly ground pepper

rocket leaves, chopped, to serve
extra olive oil and lemon juice, for dressing
shaved Parmigiano-Reggiano, to serve

* Quinoa is a pulse from South America and is an excellent source of protein.

1. Preheat the oven to 180°C/350°F/Gas Mark 4.

2. Remove all the tough outer leaves from the artichokes and trim the stems. Cut in half lengthways and remove the choke. Drizzle the cut side with the lemon juice and olive oil. Season with the salt and pepper, then press the cut sides back together with a good-sized sprig of thyme between them. Wrap individually in foil, place in the oven and cook for 40 minutes or until tender.

3. To make the salad, place the quinoa in a saucepan and cover with at least 250 ml/9 fl oz water. Bring to the boil, reduce the heat and simmer until the grains just start to swell and become tender, approximately 10–15 minutes. Drain and cool. Pound the garlic with the basil in a mortar, add the lemon juice and olive oil and mix to combine. Toast the linseeds, pumpkin seeds, sunflower seeds and pine nuts in a dry frying pan until golden, then, while still warm, toss with the basil dressing and the quinoa. Season to taste.

4. Dress the rocket with a drizzle of olive oil and a squeeze of lemon juice.

5. Unwrap the artichokes and arrange on serving plates. Scatter with the seed salad, dressed rocket and Parmigiano-Reggiano and serve.

Ben O'Donoghue

Mille-feuille of asparagus, Parmigiano-Reggiano and shaved black truffle

Spring is always heralded by the sight of wonderful fresh asparagus at the greengrocers. Here is a recipe that is a little bit decadent but still quite simple. Try to use the winter black truffles as they have more flavour than summer truffles.

SERVES 4

Vinaigrette

1$\frac{1}{2}$ tablespoons tarragon vinegar

3 tablespoons sunflower oil

2 tablespoons extra virgin olive oil

2 x 10 g/$\frac{1}{2}$ oz black truffles, shaved

24 sprigs of chervil, finely chopped

36 asparagus spears, trimmed and halved
    lengthwise

150 g/5$\frac{1}{2}$ oz Parmigiano-Reggiano, grated

100 g/3$\frac{1}{2}$ oz mixed baby herbs

100 g/3$\frac{1}{2}$ oz mixed salad leaves (wild rocket,
    endive)

1. Preheat the oven to 200°C/400°F/Gas Mark 6.

2. To make the vinaigrette, place the vinegar in a large mixing bowl and gradually add the sunflower oil, whisking constantly. Slowly add the extra virgin olive oil while continuing to whisk. Chop a quarter of the truffles and add to the vinaigrette with half the chervil. Set aside.

3. Blanch the asparagus in boiling salted water for 1 minute or until tender. Remove, refresh in ice-cold water and once cold, drain.

4. Line a baking tray with baking paper and evenly sprinkle over the Parmigiano-Reggiano. Place in the oven for 4–5 minutes or until the cheese is lacy and golden. Remove from the oven and allow to cool. Break into pieces.

5. Toss the asparagus, baby herbs, remaining chopped chervil and salad leaves in a little of the vinaigrette. On each serving plate create a stack, alternating the asparagus salad, cheese and shaved truffles. Drizzle with the remaining vinaigrette and serve.

Curtis Stone

Spiced vegetable salad with tahini dressing

Ras el hanout *mean 'top of the shop', and in Morocco it is pretty much the crème de la crème of spice mixes. With a mix containing dried rose petals, it's fantastic over a vegetable salad.*

SERVES 4

700 g/1¹⁄₂ lb pumpkin, peeled and
    cut into 1.5 cm/¹⁄₂ in slices
2 large carrots, peeled and cut
    diagonally into 1 cm/¹⁄₃ in slices
2 baby leeks
1 large eggplant (aubergine),
    cut into 1.5 cm/¹⁄₂ in wedges
60 ml/2 fl oz sunflower oil, for tossing
extra sunflower oil, for frying
4 small field mushrooms,
    about 250g/9 oz, quartered
sea salt and freshly ground black pepper

Tahini dressing

2 garlic cloves
3 tablespoons tahini
juice of 1 lemon
2 tablespoons warm water
sea salt and freshly ground pepper

1 tablespoon ras el hanout*
1 garlic clove, crushed
2 tablespoons lemon juice
1–2 teaspoons dried rose petals**

*Ras el hanout is a Moroccan blend of 23 spices
available from specialist shops.
**Dried rose petals are available from spice specialists
and online.*

1. Preheat the oven to 180°C/350°F/Gas Mark 4.

2. Boil the pumpkin until just cooked and set aside to cool.

3. Place carrots in a saucepan of boiling water, cook until tender and set aside.

4. Blanch the baby leeks until tender. Refresh in cold water.

5. Toss the eggplant in the sunflower oil then roast in the oven until golden brown.

6. Heat a little of the extra sunflower oil in a frying pan over medium heat, add the mushrooms and fry until soft. Season and set aside to cool.

7. To make the tahini dressing, pound the garlic into a paste in a mortar, mix in the tahini, then the lemon juice and finally the water. Season to taste with salt and pepper.

8. Heat a little more sunflower oil in a large, deep frying pan over a medium heat, add the ras el hanout and cook until fragrant. Add the garlic, cook briefly, and toss in the carrot, leeks, pumpkin, eggplant and mushrooms, turning carefully to coat with the spices. Cook for 2–3 minutes and squeeze over the lemon juice.

9. Arrange the vegetables on a large serving platter, top with the rose petals, dress with the tahini dressing and serve.

Pan-fried barramundi fillets with artichokes done three ways

I simply love artichokes and there are so many ways to cook them! This dish shows just how adaptable they are and what different flavours can come from the same ingredient. It certainly cuts down the shopping list!

SERVES 4

Artichoke sauce

4 tablespoons olive oil

4 x 175 g/6 oz artichokes, trimmed

300 ml/10^1/2 fl oz chicken stock

juice of ^{1}/2 lemon

Braised artichokes

90 ml/3^1/4 fl oz olive oil

2 small shallot (eschalot), finely chopped

1 large garlic clove, finely chopped

^{1}/2 carrot, peeled and sliced

8 small artichokes, trimmed and
    quartered

1.1 L/1 pint 18 ^{3}/4 fl oz chicken stock

50 g/2 oz wild rocket

Artichoke garnish

4 small artichokes, trimmed

juice of 1 lemon

2^1/2 tablespoons olive oil

sea salt and freshly ground black pepper

1 tablespoon finely chopped flat leaf parsley

4 x 180 g/6^1/4 oz fillets of barramundi,
    skin off

1 To make the artichoke sauce, heat 1 tablespoon of the olive oil in a large saucepan, add the artichokes and sauté until lightly brown. Add the chicken stock and cook for 20 minutes. Drain, reserving ^{1}/2 cup of the stock. Transfer the artichokes and the reserved stock to a food processor and process until smooth. Drizzle the remaining 3 tablespoons of olive oil down the funnel while the motor is running. Transfer to a saucepan and whisk in the lemon juice over a low heat until the sauce becomes quite thick and resembles custard in consistency.

2 To make the braised artichokes, heat 1 tablespoon of the olive oil in a heavy-based saucepan, add the shallot, garlic and carrot and sweat for 1 minute. Add the artichokes and sauté for 1 minute. Add the stock and simmer for 8–12 minutes until the artichokes are just tender. Remove the artichokes and reduce the liquid to a thick syrup (approximately 5 tablespoons). Whisk in the remaining 3^1/2 tablespoons of olive oil. Return the artichokes to the pan, add the rocket and quickly toss to combine.

continued over...

Curtis Stone

③ To make the artichoke garnish, using a mandoline, slice the artichokes as thinly as possible. Combine the lemon juice with the olive oil and whisk well. Toss through the sliced artichokes and season with salt, pepper and parsley.

④ Heat a large non-stick frying pan over medium high heat, add the fish, and cook for 3–4 minutes. Turn and cook for a further 30 seconds.

⑤ Arrange the braised artichokes in the middle of four serving plates and place the fish on top. Garnish with the sliced artichokes, drizzle the artichoke sauce around the plate and serve.

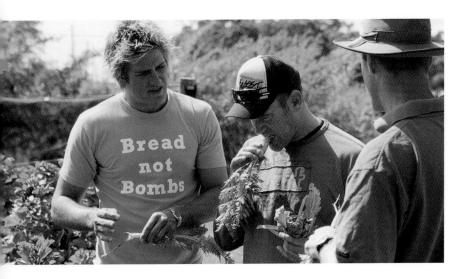

Curtis Stone

Whole roasted mullaway

I've used a whole mulloway for this version but you could also choose sliver bream.

SERVES 4–6

1.5 kg/3 lb 5 oz whole mullaway,
*   scaled, gutted and gills removed*
3 medium fennel bulbs, thinly sliced
4 shallots (eschalots), thinly sliced
1 tablespoon fennel seeds
2 garlic cloves, thinly sliced
2 lemons, sliced into thin rounds
4–6 fresh bay leaves
sea salt and freshly ground black pepper
olive oil, to drizzle
1 tablespoon rock salt
250 ml/9 fl oz dry white wine
squeeze of lemon juice
spinach, to serve

1. Preheat the oven to 180°C/350°F/Gas Mark 4.

2. Rinse the fish in cold running water and pat dry with paper towel.

3. Scatter two-thirds of the sliced fennel and shallots and all of the fennel seeds into the base of a roasting pan large enough to hold the fish. Place the fish on top and stuff the cavity with the garlic, the remaining sliced fennel and shallots, half the lemon slices and 1 bay leaf. Season with salt and pepper. Garnish the top of the fish with the remaining lemon slices and bay leaf. Drizzle over a little olive oil and season with the rock salt.

4. Place in the oven and bake for 15 minutes. Reduce the oven temperature to 150°C/300°F/ Gas Mark 2. Pour the white wine into the pan and cook for a further 10 minutes. Remove the fish from the pan, place on a plate and add a drizzle of olive oil and a squeeze of lemon juice and allow to cool to room temperature.

5. Wash the spinach and put in a hot pan with a lid. Cook until just wilted. Drain and cool. Dress with olive oil and a squeeze of lemon juice.

6. Divide the sliced fennel from the roasting pan between serving plates. Take pieces of fish off the bone and place on top of the fennel. Top with a slice of roasted lemon and a bay leaf and drizzle with juices from the roasting tray. Serve with the spinach.

Poached lamb loin with field mushrooms and cabbage with pinot noir sauce

Poaching meat and fish is a light and healthy way of cooking. If you use a flavour-filled stock as your cooking liquid, you will also transfer some of that lovely flavour to the meat.

SERVES 4

Poaching liquid

1 carrot, roughly chopped
1 celery stick, roughly chopped
2 garlic cloves, chopped
1 shallot (eschalot), chopped
1 L/1 ^{3}/4 pints veal stock
4 x 200 g/7 oz lamb loins
olive oil, for searing

Sauce

1 tablespoon olive oil
2 shallots (eschalots), sliced
1 garlic clove, sliced
100 ml/3^1/2 fl oz pinot noir
100 ml/3^1/2 fl oz red port
2 sprigs of thyme
2 bay leaves
500 ml/18 fl oz veal stock

Cabbage

1 tablespoon olive oil
1 shallot (eschalot), finely sliced
1 garlic clove, crushed
^{1}/2 cabbage, thinly sliced
100 ml/3^1/2 fl oz veal stock
1 carrot, cut into matchstick-length batons
50 g/2 oz piece flat pancetta, cut into batons
sea salt and freshly ground black pepper

1. To make the poaching liquid, combine the carrot, celery, garlic, shallot and stock in a large saucepan, place on a medium to high heat and bring to the boil. Reduce the heat to low and allow to simmer for 15 minutes.

2. Sear lamb in a pan with some olive oil over a high heat until golden brown on both sides, then add to the poaching liquid for 2–5 minutes.

3. To make the sauce, heat the olive oil in a saucepan over medium heat, add the shallots and garlic and sweat without colouring. Add the pinot noir, red port, thyme and bay leaves and simmer until reduced by half. Add the stock and reduce until it reaches a consistency where the sauce will coat the back of a spoon.

4. To make the cabbage, heat the olive oil in a large deep-sided frying pan, add the shallot and garlic and sweat for 30 seconds. Add the cabbage and stir until softened and beginning to stick to the bottom of the pan. Add the stock and simmer for 5–10 minutes.

continued opposite...

Curtis Stone

Mushrooms

1 tablespoon olive oil

$\frac{1}{2}$ shallot (eschalot), finely sliced

1 garlic clove, crushed

4 large field mushrooms, sliced

2 teaspoons finely chopped flat leaf parsley

⑤ Blanch the carrot and pancetta batons in boiling water for 60 seconds. Combine the carrot and pancetta with the cabbage, stir well, and season with salt and pepper. Remove from the heat.

⑥ To make the mushrooms, heat the olive oil in a frying pan, add the shallot and garlic and sweat for 30 seconds. Add the mushrooms and cook for 5 minutes or until soft. Add the parsley, toss well and remove from the heat.

⑦ Place the cabbage at the front of four serving plates. Stack the mushrooms at the back of the plate. Slice the lamb and place on top of the cabbage. Drizzle the sauce over the lamb and serve.

Barbecued pork belly with Ben's special sauce

Pork belly has to be the best cut of meat in the world, and cooked like this you can enjoy the full sticky indulgence that this prize cut of meat has to offer. And if you're a rum fan you will be doubly in luck.

SERVES 4–6

2–3 kg/4^1/2–6 lb 9^3/4 oz pork belly,
   rib bone end
2 L/3^1/2 pints Coca Cola
2 star anise
1 cinnamon stick

Marinade
500 g/1 lb 2 oz sugar
500 ml/18 fl oz malt vinegar
4 dried red chillies
2 cinnamon sticks
200 ml/7 fl oz tomato sauce
200 ml/7 fl oz HP sauce
100 g/3^1/2 oz creamed horseradish
100 ml/3^1/2 fl oz dark rum

^{1}/2 bunch of coriander, leaves picked
2–3 green chillies, seeded and sliced

1. Preheat the oven to 180°C/350°F/Gas Mark 4.

2. Place the pork belly in a large, deep, flameproof roasting dish over medium heat and slowly pour in enough Coca Cola to cover. Bring to the boil. Add the star anise and cinnamon stick and transfer to the oven for 2^1/2 hours or until very tender. Remove pork from the liquid and cool slightly. Discard liquid.

3. To make the marinade, combine the sugar and enough water to make a thick paste in a saucepan and cook over a medium heat until it becomes a golden colour. Remove from the heat and carefully add the malt vinegar, chillies and cinnamon sticks. Cook until the mixture has reduced to the consistency it was before the vinegar was added. Add the tomato sauce and HP sauce and reduce to the original consistency again. Stir in the horseradish and rum. Remove from the heat immediately and allow to cool.

4. Place the pork belly in a large ceramic dish, pour over the marinade. Cover pork with cling wrap, and set aside in the refrigerator for 2–3 hours.

continued opposite...

5. Preheat a covered barbecue* (preferably a coal burner) to medium. Cook the pork belly with the cover down for 10–15 minutes, basting during cooking with the marinade it was resting in.

6. To serve, slice the pork belly and arrange on a serving platter, sprinkle over the coriander and chillies and brush with any remaining sauce.

*If you don't have a covered barbecue, you can cook the pork belly in a 200°C/400°F/Gas Mark 6 oven.

Strawberry spring rolls

I love spring rolls, but to succeed they must be very thin. You could also try pate de brik, which is a North African pastry.

SERVES 8

Strawberry filling

2 punnets strawberries, hulled

*¹/₂ bunch of mint, leaves picked and
    finely sliced*

2 tablespoons icing sugar, plus extra to dust

freshly ground black pepper

40 wonton wrappers

1 egg white, lightly beaten

sunflower oil, to deep-fry

100 g/3¹/₄ oz dark chocolate, melted

*double/thick cream, ice-cream or vanilla
    yoghurt, to serve*

extra strawberries, to serve

1. To make the strawberry filling, chop the strawberries and mix with the mint, icing sugar and a grind of black pepper.

2. Place a wonton wrapper on a chopping board and spread 2 teaspoons of the strawberry filling along the bottom side of the wrapper. Fold and roll over once, then fold in either end and roll almost completely. Wet the end of the wonton wrapper with a little egg white to seal. Repeat with the remaining wrappers and filling.

3. Half fill a large wok or saucepan with the sunflower oil and heat to 180°C/350°F*. Cook in small batches for 2–3 minutes or until crisp and golden. Drain on paper towel.

4. Divide the spring rolls between serving plates and dust with icing sugar. Drizzle over melted chocolate and serve with cream, ice-cream or vanilla yoghurt.

**If you don't have a thermometer, drop in a small piece
of bread, which will fry to golden brown in 1 minute
at the correct temperature.*

Red berry soup with champagne sorbet

This soup is fantastic for summer because it is light and refreshing. Some of my mates would come into my restaurant in London and not want to finish the night with a port or sweet wine. So I dreamed up this dish for Jo and Ruthie so they could keep drinking champagne and come out partying.

SERVES 4

250 g/9 oz strawberries
250 g/9 oz raspberries
250 g/9 oz blackberries
250 g/9 oz blueberries
25 g/1 oz icing sugar
*4 scoops champagne sorbet**

1 Set aside 50 g/2 oz of each berry for the garnish.

2 Place the remaining berries in a large heatproof bowl with the icing sugar and cover with plastic wrap. Place the bowl over a saucepan of simmering water and allow to steam for 45 minutes. Remove from the heat and pour through a fine strainer, allowing the juice to drip through for 20 minutes. Discard the berries. Transfer the soup to the refrigerator to chill.

3 To serve, pour the soup into four glass serving bowls. Place a ball of champagne sorbet in each bowl and garnish with the reserved berries.

*If champagne sorbet is unavailable, substitute with good quality vanilla ice-cream.

Curtis Stone

Cairns Highlands

Cairns Highlands

Where the rainforest meets the sea

Cairns is above the Tropic of Capricorn on the east coast of Australia between Brisbane and Cape York. Known as the gateway to the Great Barrier Reef, its climate is tropical and, not surprisingly, ideal for growing tropical fruits, especially bananas and mangoes, vegetables and sugar.

The Cairns Highlands (Atherton Tablelands) is the food-bowl of Far North Queensland for the markets down south. The tablelands feature rich red volcanic soils with many deep freshwater lakes contained in the craters of extinct volcanoes.

We arrived at Cairns Airport to wait for our lift — a helicopter to go fishing! We took off and were soon flying over untouched rainforest, pure blue lakes and a patchwork of rich red-soiled farms.

We swooped low through a spectacular rainforest, past waterfalls and down wild ravines. The chopper put us down deep in the rainforest, many kilometres from any road or track, landing on a ledge of crazy-paving volcanic rock. Ben caught the first fish, a mountain bream, about 2 kilograms in weight. It was a beautiful fish, which we cooked later, wrapped in banana leaves.

We then went to a secluded beach where Captain Cook's ship *Endeavour* was beached for repairs in the 1770s. Captain Cook looms large in Australia's history as the man who claimed the continent for the British. Even though Aboriginal people have been here for tens of thousands of years, the English sailors who were trapped on the beach by thick rainforest could not recognise any food to eat. We wandered into the rainforest and were immediately caught up in a prickly vine. But we had been told what to look for and were able to find some indigenous Davidson plums and lemon aspen fruit. They'd have kept you alive but they're not the most edible fruit, being both tart and astringent in flavour. Think lemon, then triple it.

We next flew low over lush green sugarcane fields, their fronds, under the influence of the chopper's blades, dancing like the ocean's waves. Cane sugar is one of the main crops of the region. Raw sugar is Australia's second largest export crop. Each year Queensland exports some four million tonnes, which is about 80 per cent of the total it produces.

A little cane train took us to the historic and rustic Gordonvale sugar mill. Each hopper being pulled by the train contains 4 tonnes of raw cane and is delivered to the mill no later than sixteen hours after harvest to keep quality up. Steam spouted from the Gordonvale mill's doors, smoke billowed from its chimneys and the thump, thump, thump of ancient machinery could be heard and felt. A giant swivel hopper unloaded rough cane stalks. The cane then goes into the plant where it is crushed. For every 7 tonnes of raw cane, a single tonne of sugar is produced. The sugar at this stage is syrup. It is then grown into sugar crystals. The sugar is completely natural.

But this plant is virtually self-sustaining. The residue of the cane is used to fire the boilers and run the turbines. Not only does it run the plant, there's also enough electricity left over to be put back into the grid and power 4000 local homes.

Flying low across lush pastureland, we saw a herd of buffalo. Later, we dropped in for a chat with Mitchell Humphries, an organic farmer who keeps buffalo for milk to make traditional mozzarella cheese.

We next flew low over a huge plantation of bananas and decided to drop in for a visit. But it wasn't just bananas they produced; this was the Mount Uncle Distillery which also makes an incredible range of liqueurs. We went out to harvest some bananas, which is not as easy as it looks. Basically, using a sharp cane knife, a slash is made about 2 metres above and as the plant falls you're meant to catch the tail of the banana bunch and in a single motion, cut it from its stem. These bunches are bloody heavy, too. We had a go, but none of those boys needs to worry about his job.

The banana plant has a huge vascular system that pumps water right through its trunk directly into the banana bunch. Another interesting fact is that when the trunk (known as the mother plant) is cut down, it's cut up and left to break down and enrich the soil. On either side of the mother plant a 'daughter plant' will soon sprout and the whole process starts all over again.

Another surprise up that way was to come across a huge Glen Allyn tea plantation. Not a crop usually associated with Australia.

The tea plant is *Camellia sinensis,* which is related to the flowering camellia. The top 75 to 100 millimetres of new growth is taken off every 17 to 21 days in the hottest season and every 28 to 30 in the cooler months. Camellia bushes can continue to produce for up to 100 years! This tea is grown without the use of pesticides, as it has no natural predators there. Interestingly, the taste and caffeine content of tea varies throughout the year. And the fresher the tea, the better the flavour.

Salad of witlof and blue cheese with roasted walnuts

Witlof, or endive, can be quite a bitter leaf. So to match its flavour with a strong, salty cheese and the rich flavour of walnuts makes for a perfect balance.

SERVES 4

Dressing

40 g/1$\frac{1}{2}$ oz Roquefort or similar firm
   blue cheese
2$\frac{1}{2}$ tablespoons tarragon vinegar
100 ml/3$\frac{1}{2}$ fl oz sunflower oil
4 tablespoons extra virgin olive oil
3 teaspoons chopped chives
freshly ground white pepper

Salad

2 red witlof, trimmed
3 white witlof, trimmed
120 g/4$\frac{1}{4}$ oz blue cheese, crumbled
150 g/5$\frac{1}{2}$ oz walnuts, roasted and
   roughly chopped

1. To make the dressing, crumble the blue cheese into a large mixing bowl. Add the vinegar and whisk into a smooth paste. Slowly add the sunflower oil and extra virgin olive oil, whisking constantly. Add the chives and season with the pepper.

2. To assemble the salad, separate the witlof leaves and cut lengthways into 1 cm/$\frac{1}{2}$ in strips. Mix the shredded witlof with the cheese and walnuts and drizzle over enough dressing to coat the salad. Serve in a large bowl.

Curtis Stone

Risotto of freshwater crayfish with green peas

The beauty of risotto is that it's just as easy to make it for ten people as it is for two. So invite a few more friends around! This recipe is also very adaptable: if you can't find freshwater crays, you could use prawns or any other shellfish for that matter.

SERVES 4

1 tablespoon olive oil

2$\frac{1}{2}$ shallots (eschalots), finely diced

2$\frac{1}{2}$ garlic cloves, finely chopped

3 sprigs of thyme

400 g/14 oz Vialone Nano rice

175ml/6$\frac{1}{4}$ fl oz white wine

1.2 L/2 pints chicken or vegetable stock, warmed

125 g/4$\frac{1}{2}$ oz small green peas

115 g/4$\frac{1}{4}$ oz butter

flesh of 4 medium-sized freshwater crayfish, chopped

squeeze of lemon juice

40 g/1$\frac{1}{2}$ oz Parmigiano-Reggiano cheese

40 g/1$\frac{1}{2}$ oz mascarpone cheese

1$\frac{1}{2}$ tablespoons finely chopped flat leaf parsley

sea salt and freshly ground black pepper

4 sprigs of chervil, to garnish

1. Heat the olive oil in a medium heavy-based saucepan over a medium heat. Add the shallots, garlic and thyme and sweat for 1 minute, without colouring. Add the rice and sweat for 30 seconds. Pour in the wine and cook until it is absorbed. Add 1 ladleful of stock and cook, stirring constantly, until absorbed. Continue adding the stock, ladle by ladle, until all has been absorbed. This should take about 20 minutes. Add the peas and continue to cook for 30–60 seconds. The rice should be cooked to the point of being *al dente* (the centre of each grain of rice should be slightly firm to the tooth).

2. Melt 25 g/1 oz of the butter in a separate saucepan, add the crayfish and toss the pan for 30 seconds. Add a squeeze of the lemon juice to taste.

3. Add half of the crayfish to the risotto, reserving the other half for the garnish, and stir. Remove from the heat, add the Parmigiano-Reggiano, the mascarpone and the remaining butter and stir until the butter has melted. Add the parsley and season.

4. Divide the risotto between four warmed serving bowls, garnish with the reserved crayfish and a sprig of chervil and serve.

Curtis Stone

Barbecued skewers of mozzarella, pancetta and radicchio

Most people think of pizza or melts when they cook with mozzarella, but the flavours of smoky pancetta, crispy olive oil-drenched bread, and the fresh sharpness of mozzarella in these skewers is wonderful. Just cook them quickly on a hot grill or barbecue.

SERVES 4

8 long thick rosemary stalks

4 x 100 g/3½ oz balls of fresh mozzarella*
1 garlic clove, finely chopped
4 tablespoons extra virgin olive oil
day-old sourdough or ciabatta bread,
    cut into 16 3-cm/1¼-in cubes
16 slices of pancetta, cut into thin strips
1 head of radicchio
1 tablespoon aged balsamic vinegar,
    plus extra to serve
sea salt and freshly ground black pepper
handful of toasted pine nuts, to serve
shaved parmesan, to serve

1. Remove the leaves from all but the ends of the rosemary stalks. Cut the mozzarella into 3-cm/1¼-in chunks.

2. Mix the garlic with 3 tablespoons of the olive oil and toss the cubes of bread in the flavoured oil.

3. Wrap the bread cubes in the strips of pancetta and thread onto the rosemary stems, alternating with the mozzarella chunks. You should have two pieces of mozzarella and bread on each stem.

4. Slice the radicchio into thin wedges and barbecue to wilt the leaves, approximately 2 minutes. Toss with the remaining olive oil, the balsamic vinegar, salt and pepper.

5. Preheat the barbecue or grill. Chargrill the skewers on the barbecue or grill, turning every minute and grilling each side twice. Take care not to overcook, or the mozzarella will melt too much.

6. Place the radicchio and two skewers on each serving plate. Drizzle with a little extra balsamic vinegar, sprinkle over the pine nuts and shaved parmesan and serve.

*Note. If you can't find fresh mozzarella, use 8 bocconcini, halved.

Pan-fried pearl perch with horseradish sauce

Horseradish is usually served with beef, but it is also surprisingly good with fish. It has a strong flavour so don't overcomplicate the dish. All I serve it with is a little spinach.

SERVES 4

2 tablespoons olive oil

4 shallots (eschalots), sliced

1 sprig of thyme

2 bay leaves

250 ml/9 fl oz white wine

250 ml/9 fl oz Noilly Prat dry vermouth

250 ml/9 fl oz fish stock

300 ml/10^1/2 fl oz pouring cream

1 scant tablespoon horseradish,
    finely grated

1 tablespoon finely chopped flat
    leaf parsley

4 x 200 g/7 oz pearl perch or
    barramundi fillets, skin on

sea salt and freshly ground black pepper

50 g/2 oz butter

squeeze of lemon juice

300 g/11 oz baby spinach

mixed baby herbs dressed with olive oil,
    to garnish

1 Heat 1 tablespoon of the olive oil in a saucepan over medium heat. Add the shallots, thyme and bay leaves and sweat, without colouring, for 1 minute. Add the white wine and over a low heat reduce to a syrup, approximately 3 tablespoons. Add the Noilly Prat and again reduce to a syrup. Then add the fish stock and reduce to a syrup once more. Add the cream and bring to a soft simmer. Remove from the heat and strain.

2 Gently warm the strained sauce and slowly add the horseradish to taste (horseradish varies in strength depending on its freshness). Add the parsley, cover, and keep warm.

3 Heat the remaining 1 tablespoon of olive oil in a non-stick frying pan over medium to high heat.

4 Season the fish with salt and pepper and place, skin-side down, in the pan. Cook for 2–3 minutes, turn and cook for a further 30 seconds. Add a nob of the butter and the lemon juice and baste the fish with the juices in the pan.

5 Melt the remaining butter in a separate pan, add the baby spinach, season with salt and pepper and cook over a low heat until just wilted. Drain.

6 Place a mound of spinach in the centre of four warmed serving plates. Position a perch fillet on top, drizzle the sauce around the outside of the plate and serve.

Curtis Stone

Native perch baked in banana leaf with yoghurt, mint and chilli

You don't really have to use a banana leaf, foil will do! The combination of the mint, yoghurt and chilli really pick up the flavours of fatty fish like these native perch. Or you could just as easily substitute lobster or large prawns.

SERVES 4

4 x 450 g/1 lb whole perch or
similar fish (e.g. baby barramundi),
scaled, gutted and gills removed
500 ml/18 fl oz natural yoghurt
1/2 bunch of mint, leaves picked
2–3 dried chillies, roughly chopped
juice and finely grated zest of 1 lemon
4 banana leaves, to wrap fish
500 g/1 lb 2 oz baby zucchini (courgette)
1 garlic clove, crushed
1–2 tablespoons white wine vinegar
1–2 tablespoons olive oil
sea salt and freshly ground black pepper
extra virgin olive oil, to drizzle
mint leaves, to garnish

1. Preheat the barbecue to medium high or the oven to 200°C/400°F/Gas Mark 6.

2. Place the yoghurt, mint, chillies, lemon juice and zest in a blender and process until smooth.

3. Coat the fish in the yoghurt mixture, and place each fish on a banana leaf. Cover each fish with any remaining yoghurt mixture. Wrap and secure the banana leaves with skewers or kitchen twine. Place straight on the coals of the barbecue (turn occasionally), or into the oven, for 10 minutes. Remove and allow to rest for 3 minutes.

4. Boil the whole baby zucchini until just tender. Drain and roughly chop, then mix with the garlic, vinegar, olive oil, salt and pepper.

5. To serve, place the banana leaf on a plate and open. Surround fish with baby zucchini, drizzle with extra virgin olive oil and garnish with mint leaves.

Poached venison with creamed corn, mushrooms and red wine sauce

I cook this dish at The Atlantic where we use a very reduced veal stock to poach the meat, but at home a rich thick gravy will do the job just as well.

SERVES 4

Creamed corn

3–4 corn on the cob or 3 cups kibbled corn
300 ml/10$\frac{1}{2}$ fl oz double/thick cream
1 garlic clove, crushed
lime juice, to taste
sea salt and freshly ground black pepper

Poaching liquid

1 L/1$\frac{3}{4}$ pints red wine (cabernet or merlot)
$\frac{1}{2}$ bunch of thyme
1 tablespoon peppercorns
2 garlic cloves, finely chopped
4 tablespoons gravy powder

4 x 180 g/6$\frac{1}{4}$ oz venison loin portions
1 tablespoon butter, to sauté
4 large slippery jack or medium field
    mushrooms or pine mushrooms, sliced
Flat-leaf parsley, finely chopped, for garnish

1. To make the creamed corn, boil the corn on the cob in salted water until tender. Cool slightly and cut the kernels from the cob. Reserve $\frac{1}{2}$ cup of the kernels, placing the rest in a saucepan. Add the cream and garlic, bring to a simmer and cook until reduced and thickened slightly. Puree until smooth but still quite thick, stir in the reserved whole kernels and season with a little lime juice, salt and pepper.

2. To make the poaching liquid, bring the red wine to the boil in a saucepan and add the thyme, peppercorns and garlic. Cook, uncovered, until reduced by a quarter. Mix a little of the liquid with the gravy powder to make a smooth paste, then add to the pan. Simmer until thickened enough to coat the back of a spoon. Add more gravy powder if needed.

3. Place the portions of venison in the poaching liquid and cook gently for 8–10 minutes, turning every few minutes. Set aside and cover loosely with foil for 2 minutes, to rest.

4. Sauté the mushrooms in butter for approximately 2 minutes, or until golden.

continued opposite...

5 To serve, place a large spoonful of creamed corn on each warmed plate and top with mushroom slices crisscrossed over each other. Sprinkle with the chopped parsley. Slice the venison, place on the side of the plate and coat with the red wine sauce.

Ben O'Donoghue

Tea-smoked organic duck salad

Smoking is an interesting way to incorporate flavour into food. Here is a simple way to do it at home. This is a technique that, once you have experimented with it at home, will have you hooked. You can smoke anything from oysters to mozzarella using a range of smoke flavours derived from dried mushrooms to hickory chips.

SERVES 4

2 x 200 g/7 oz organic duck breasts
2 teaspoons rock salt
1 teaspoon smoked paprika
10 g/$^1/_3$ oz dried shiitake mushrooms
100 g/3$^1/_2$ oz Earl Grey tea leaves
1 tablespoon olive oil

Vinaigrette

2$^1/_2$ tablespoons balsamic vinegar
4 tablespoons grape seed oil
1 tablespoon extra virgin olive oil
sea salt and freshly ground black pepper

20 g /$^2/_3$ oz mixed baby herbs
20 g/$^2/_3$ oz wild rocket
10 g/$^1/_3$ oz watercress
3 oranges, segmented
2$^1/_2$ tablespoons honey

1. Rub the duck breasts with the rock salt and smoked paprika and refrigerate for 1 hour to marinate.

2. Place the duck breasts in a steamer that fits over a heavy-based saucepan with a tight-fitting lid. Heat the saucepan on high until red hot. Add the dried mushrooms and tea leaves, and immediately place the steamer containing the duck breasts on top and cover. Turn off the heat and allow the smoke to infuse the duck breasts for 5 minutes. Repeat this process.

3. Heat the olive oil in a frying pan over a medium heat, add the duck and allow the fat to render down for 45 seconds while colouring the skin to a nice golden brown. Allow the duck to rest for 1 minute.

4. To make the vinaigrette, whisk the balsamic vinegar in a mixing bowl and gradually add the grape seed oil and extra virgin olive oil. Taste the dressing and season with salt and pepper.

5. Combine the baby herbs, rocket and watercress and dress with the vinaigrette, reserving a little to drizzle over the finished dish.

continued opposite...

6. Toss the orange segments in the honey and mix through the dressed salad leaves. Place in the centre of each serving plate.

7. Thinly slice the duck breasts and arrange on the salad. Drizzle the reserved vinaigrette around the outside of each plate and serve.

Roast duck salad with lychees, pomelo and crispy onion

The Chinese are simply the best at cooking duck. The real secret is to choose a duck with a high amount of fat, then to dry it out well and roast it slowly. Or just buy one from a Chinatown near you! The combination of citrus and sweet lychees is a perfect accompaniment.

SERVES 6–8

1.8 kg/3 lb 15$^{1}/_{2}$ oz duck*
2 tablespoons maltose
2 tablespoons hoisin sauce
2 tablespoons Shaoxing rice wine**
1 teaspoon Chinese five-spice powder
2 teaspoons sugar
2 teaspoons salt
1 large onion, sliced
sunflower oil, for frying
12 fresh lychees, peeled and seeded
1 pomelo, peeled and segmented
$^{1}/_{2}$ bunch of mint, leaves picked
sesame oil, for dressing

1. Remove the fat, skin, wings and parson's nose from the duck then plunge into boiling water for 10 minutes. Scrape away any visible fat and bubbles and pat dry with paper towel.

2. Combine the maltose, hoisin sauce and the Shaoxing rice wine in a saucepan over a medium heat and bring to the boil. Add the five-spice powder at boiling point and continue to boil for 1 minute, then remove from the heat and allow to cool.

3. Place the duck in a large ceramic dish and brush all over with the hoisin mixture. Place in the fridge for 24 hours to allow the duck to dry out. Reserve any remaining marinade for the salad.

4. Preheat the oven to 180°C/350°F/Gas Mark 4.

5. Place the duck in the oven and roast for 1 hour. Set aside to cool. Remove the breasts and legs, reserve.

continued over...

*You could buy an already-cooked Chinese barbecued duck if you like.
**Shaoxing rice wine is a traditional Chinese yellow rice wine. If unavailable, dry sherry or vermouth may be substituted.

Roast duck salad with lychees, pomelo and crispy onion, continued ...

6) Sprinkle the sugar and salt over the onion and set aside to allow the liquid to be drawn out. Squeeze dry. Heat the sunflower oil to 140°C/275°F in a wok and fry the onion until crisp and golden.

7) Slice the breasts and legs and return to a warm oven, for no more than 5 minutes.

8) Toss the lychees and pomelo with the mint and arrange on serving plates. Divide the duck meat between each plate and drizzle over reserved hoisin marinade as a dressing. Sprinkle over the crispy onion and a little sesame oil and serve.

Ben O'Donoghue

Chocolate tart with organic yoghurt

This is quite a classic chocolate tart, lightened up with the use of organic yoghurt.

SERVES 8

Pastry

100 g/3¹/₂ oz butter, diced

100 g/3¹/₂ oz icing sugar

2 eggs

250 g/9 oz plain flour

pinch of salt

Filling

5 eggs

90 g/3¹/₄ oz sugar

190 g/6³/₄ oz butter, melted

290 g/10¹/₄ oz dark chocolate, 70 per cent
    cocoa solids, melted

natural organic yoghurt, to serve

① To make the pastry, place the butter and icing sugar in a mixing bowl and beat for 2 minutes. Add the eggs, one at a time, and beat for 2 minutes or until smooth. Slowly add the flour and salt and mix until the dough just comes together. Wrap in plastic wrap and rest in the refrigerator overnight.

② Preheat the oven to 200°C/400°F/Gas Mark 6.

③ On a lightly floured bench, roll out the pastry to 3 mm/⅛ in thick. Invert the pastry into a lightly greased 20 cm/8 in springform tin to line the inside and base, allowing the pastry to overhang the rim of the tin.

④ Place a piece of baking paper over the pastry and fill with baking weights or rice. Place in the oven and bake blind for 10–15 minutes. Remove from the oven and discard the paper and rice.

⑤ Reduce oven temperature to 150°C/300°F/Gas Mark 2. Return the tin to the oven for 5 minutes.

⑥ To make the filling, place the eggs and sugar in a mixing bowl and beat for 5 minutes or until the mixture is quite stiff.

continued over...

Chocolate tart with organic yoghurt, continued...

7. Meanwhile, combine the butter and chocolate and mix well. Gently fold a third of the chocolate mixture at a time into the egg mixture. Be careful not to over mix.

8. Pour the filling into the pastry case and bake for 10–15 minutes. Allow to cool to room temperature.

9. Cut into slices with a hot knife and serve with the yoghurt.

Curtis Stone

Vanilla tapioca with tropical fruits

Tapioca is one off those things your mother might have cooked for you but burnt, and so put you off for life. My mission is to convert any of those unfortunate souls. Tapioca — sometimes revoltingly called frogs' spawn — is sensational. Coupled with lush tropical fruits you can't lose.

SERVES 8

300 g/11 oz tapioca
600 ml/1 pint water
500 ml/18 fl oz pouring cream
500 ml/18 fl oz milk
2 vanilla pods, split lengthways
10 egg yolks
200 g/7 oz caster sugar
tropical fruit (mangoes, passionfruit,
*   kiwifruit, bananas and lychees),*
*   to serve*

1. Place the tapioca in a mixing bowl, add the water and set aside in a warm place for 1 hour. It will swell a little. Drain and rinse thoroughly.

2. Combine the cream, milk and vanilla pods in a saucepan over medium to high heat. Bring just to the boil and add the tapioca. Reduce the heat slightly and cook for about 15 minutes or until the tapioca is soft and transparent and the mixture is thick.

3. Whisk the egg yolks and the sugar together until combined. Add to the tapioca and stir for 5 minutes over a low heat. Allow to cool until slightly above room temperature.

4. Serve topped with the tropical fruit.

Ben O'Donoghue

Eyre Peninsula

Eyre Peninsula

Bounty on the desert's doorstep

The Eyre Peninsula, west of Adelaide, is bound by Whyalla, Port Lincoln and, in the west, Ceduna on the Nullarbor Plain. A lot of wheat and barley is grown and exported to all points of the globe from the Eyre Peninsula and wherever you travel, you're reminded of its grain-growing heritage. Fields of wheat, barley and the bright yellow flowers of the blossoming canola crop are everywhere.

But the main harvest comes from the south, from the great Southern Ocean that has generated extraordinary wealth for migrants who emigrated here and brought with them little else than a bag full of determination and their fishing skills.

We love oysters. The fresher, the better. So when we met Lester Marshall, we knew it was going to be a great day. Lester buys oyster 'spats' that are just 3 millimetres across. He buys millions of them every year; 7 million this year alone. And under his care, and in the crystal clear waters of Coffin Bay — a beautiful bay that looks more like a lake you might find in Scotland than Australia — they grow plump, succulent and delicious.

Just waist deep in the sandy-bottomed bay, oysters sit in racks and filter minute algae and nutrients from the tidal water passing by. Because the bay has a 1-metre tide, the oysters spend 60 per cent of their time under the water and 40 per cent of their time out of it. This is their natural state. Lester harvests and sells around 230 tonnes of oysters each year.

Lester has some really big oysters as well as his regular range. We each tried one that we reckon weighed about 500 grams in the shell. To give you an idea of its size, the normal oyster we would serve in our restaurants is mostly 80 to 100 grams in the shell.

Johnny Newton is an abalone diver. And a good one too, so we went out with him in his boat to see how it's done.

Now it should be said, right up front, that some people think these guys get paid way too much money for diving for these delicacies. But there are a few things they haven't factored in:

1. in season, the divers work seven days a week; 2. it's really bloody cold in the water; and 3. they dive in shark-infested waters. Not just any sharks mind you, but Great Whites! Which is why Johnny normally dives inside a shark cage. We're not sure about abalone diving as a career choice, even if you do get to go surfing quite a lot outside of the season.

We went underwater with Johnny and the first thing we realised is that abalone are really hard to see. Covered in seaweed and clinging to a rock, they are perfectly camouflaged. You've certainly got to know what you're looking for. There are two types of abalone there: black lip and green lip. The green lip is the most prized and worth big dollars in China and Japan. Wild abalone sells at a premium rate, although more and more people are establishing abalone farms, which they believe have a big and sustainable future. To the connoisseur, the wild and farmed varieties have a different texture, although the taste, coming from the same clear, clean waters, is similar.

Johnny told us that licenses to take the abalone are passed down from father to son. Bag limits and quotas ensure the industry's future is sustainable.

However, the thing that Port Lincoln is most famous for is tuna. And these fish have made a mostly migrant community very wealthy. We were told there were more millionaires per head of population down there than anywhere else in Australia. We met one of them, Hagen Stehr, who, having made his fortune from tuna, is now pioneering the farming of kingfish (which are known as *hiramasa* in Japan) and mulloway, both growing in demand in Asia.

Tuna farming is quite amazing. First, the fishing vessels head out about 200 kilometres into the Great Australia Bight. Then a spotter plane finds where the schools of juvenile tuna are. The boats then round the fish up (like cowboys on horseback) into a large net that they draw together and join at the ends. Divers go below and join the bottom so that the tuna are now in what is essentially a giant floating fish pen. The pen is then dragged, very slowly, all the way back to the sheltered bays of Port Lincoln. Here the tuna swim within their giant pens and are fed pilchards on a regular basis. When they're big and plump, they're in great demand around the world. These tuna are the best of both worlds — wild stock, fed on their natural diet of pilchards, yet protected from predators and living in a pristine environment.

The reason why fish farming is the way of the future is simple. There are about 120 million tonnes of fish eaten around the world every year but only an estimated 100 million tonnes of new fish spawning in the same period. Wild fish are just not going to be able to satisfy demand on their own. To see the result of overfishing, just look at what happened to cod fishing in the North Sea. They were fished to virtual extinction.

We don't think twice about farming animals on the land for food, and so we're all going to have to get used to the idea of more and more of our fish coming from farms. But not all farms are equal; many in other parts of the world are in polluted waters. And in some unregulated markets, antibiotics and so forth are administered.

At least from what we've seen, if fish farming is the way of the future, then the way it's done at Port Lincoln is the best way to do it. Australia's strict quota laws may annoy some fishermen, but it certainly ensures that their children will be able to carry on fishing for a living, and their children's children, too.

Oysters with miso jelly and pickled ginger

Oysters are the food of the gods. If you don't like them raw, try eating them cooked first, then slowly include a few that are raw. It always helps to make sure they are fresh and cold. This recipe is great because the ginger and lime kick in with the flavour of the oyster.

SERVES 8

Miso jelly
15 g/¹⁄₂ oz kombu*
500 ml/18 fl oz water
15 g/¹⁄₂ oz bonito flakes
25 g/1 oz white miso
3 leaves of gelatine

Pickled ginger
250 g/9 oz young ginger, peeled and
    thinly sliced
3 tablespoons caster sugar
1 tablespoon sea salt
4 tablespoons rice wine vinegar

48 oysters in their shells

1 kg rock salt, or crushed ice, for serving
coriander cress, to garnish**
1 lime, quartered

* Kombu is dried kelp and is available from
Asian food specialists.
** Chopped coriander may be substituted if
coriander cress is unavailable.

1. To make the miso jelly, place the kombu in a saucepan, add the water and bring to just under the boil. Reduce the heat and simmer for 10 minutes. Do not boil as the kombu will make the water cloudy. Remove from the heat and discard the kombu. Add the bonito flakes and allow to stand until the flakes have sunk to the bottom. Pass through a fine sieve into a bowl and whisk in the miso. Soak the gelatine in cold water until softened, squeeze out the excess water. Dissolve in a little of the miso stock, then whisk into the remaining stock. Chill in the refrigerator until set.

2. To pickle the ginger, soak the ginger in cold water for 5 minutes, then drain. Dissolve the sugar and salt in the vinegar, pour into a saucepan and bring to the boil. Pour over the ginger and leave to cool in the liquid.

3. Open and remove the oysters from their shells and refrigerate until required. Wash and reserve the shells.

4. Arrange the oyster shells on a platter on a bed of moistened rock salt or crushed ice. With a spoon break the miso jelly. Then spoon a small amount into each oyster shell and top with an oyster. Garnish with the pickled ginger and coriander cress and serve with a wedge of lime.

Sea urchins with fennel puree and shellfish foam

These interesting little things are a delicacy in Asia. This is a great recipe as a starter or a canapé.

*12 sea urchin lobes**

Shellfish stock

2 L/3$\frac{1}{2}$ pints water
2 onions, peeled and chopped
2 carrots, peeled and chopped
1 leek, chopped
2 kg/4$\frac{1}{2}$ lb fresh clams (vongole)
1 kg/2 lb 4 oz cockles

Fennel puree

1 tablespoon olive oil
300 g/11 oz bulb of fennel, sliced
2 tablespoons Pernod
200 ml/7 fl oz fish stock
200 ml/7 fl oz shellfish stock
2$\frac{1}{2}$ tablespoons pouring cream

Shellfish foam

Remaining shellfish stock
1 tablespoon olive oil
2 shallots (eschalots), sliced
2$\frac{1}{2}$ tablespoons white wine
500 ml/18 fl oz pouring cream

*Sea urchin lobes can be purchased from fishmongers
and seafood markets

1. Rinse the lobes under water and set aside.

2. To make the shellfish stock, combine the water, onions, carrots and leek in a large saucepan and bring to the boil. Add the clams and cockles and cook for 8 minutes. Strain through a fine sieve and reserve.

3. To make the fennel puree, heat the olive oil in a saucepan over a medium heat, add the fennel and sweat for 2 minutes. Add the Pernod and once it has reduced, add the fish stock and shellfish stock. Simmer for 20 minutes or until the fennel is cooked. Strain, place the fennel in a blender and process until smooth. Add the cream, then pass the fennel puree through a fine sieve and keep warm.

4. Heat the olive oil in a saucepan over a medium heat, add the shallots and sweat until lightly coloured. Deglaze the pan with the white wine. Add the remaining shellfish stock and reduce to a glaze (it should be slightly thickened and shiny). Add the cream, bring to a simmer and strain. To finish the shellfish foam, froth the sauce with a hand blender.

5. To serve, place 1 small spoonful of fennel puree in the bottom of six warmed shot glasses. Place 2 sea urchin lobes in each glass, spoon over the shellfish foam and serve immediately.

Curtis Stone

Tempura oysters with mayonnaise and salmon roe

The best thing to do with oysters that are a little too big is to cook them. This is a great Japanese combination.

SERVES 4

$^1/_2$ cup Japanese Kupi mayonnaise*
$1^1/_2$ teaspoons mirin
2 teaspoons Shoyu soy sauce**

Batter
$^1/_4$ cup plain flour
$^1/_2$ cup ice-cold water

24 oysters, shucked
plain flour, for dusting
sunflower oil, enough for deep-frying
1 kg/2 lb 4 oz rock salt
150 ml/5$^1/_2$ fl oz water
50 g/2 oz salmon roe

① Combine the mayonnaise, mirin and soy sauce in a small bowl.

② To make the batter, place the flour in a small bowl, add the ice-cold water and lightly mix with chopsticks to make a thin, slightly lumpy batter.

③ Remove the oysters from their shells. Wash the shells, pat dry and reserve for serving. Pat the oysters dry with paper towel and lightly dust with flour.

④ Heat sunflower oil in a wok or large saucepan.

⑤ Dip the oysters into the batter, drain off the excess batter and deep-fry for 30 seconds. Drain the oysters on paper towel and place back into the shells.

⑥ Slightly moisten the rock salt with the water and spread onto four serving plates. Arrange six oysters on top so that they are sitting level. Place a dollop of the mayonnaise sauce on top of each oyster, garnish with the salmon roe and serve.

* Japanese Kupi mayonnaise can be purchased at specialist Asian food shops.
** Shoyu soy sauce is a usually sweeter, less salty soy sauce from Japan and can be purchased at specialist Asian food shops.

Curtis Stone

Tuna tartare Niçoise

This is a fresh take on the classic steak tartare. It's great as a starter but also works well on little crostini as a canapé.

SERVES 4

300 g/11 oz sushi grade tuna, diced into 5 mm/¼ in cubes
50 g/2 oz green beans, blanched and cut into 5 mm/¼ in lengths
½ potato, cooked and diced
1 small shallot (eschalot), chopped
1 tablespoon baby capers (if salted, soak in cold water for 30 minutes and rinse well)
sea salt and freshly ground black pepper
60 g/2¼ oz small, black Niçoise olives
2 tablespoons extra virgin olive oil
1 tablespoon finely chopped chives
4 lime cheeks, to serve (optional)

1. Combine the extra virgin olive oil and chives in a small bowl. Set aside.

2. Place the tuna, green beans, potato, shallot and capers in a large bowl. Season with the salt and pepper and stir to combine.

3. Place a 9 cm/3½ in round cutter on a serving plate. Spoon a quarter of the tuna mixture into the cutter and press down firmly. Gently remove the cutter and repeat on each serving plate.

4. Scatter the olives around the outside of each serving plate, drizzle with the oil, sprinkle over chives and serve with the lime cheeks.

Curtis Stone

Kingfish salad Niçoise

Seeing these fish and the careful way that they were farmed in lovely clean water gave me a great sense of reassurance. They are good for you — high in omega 3 — and taste simply brilliant. Kingfish are dark and meaty so that's why I've used them in my version of a Niçoise salad.

SERVES 4–6

750 ml/1 pint 7 fl oz olive oil
2 garlic cloves, sliced
2 anchovy fillets
750 g/1 lb 10^1/$_2$ oz king fish fillet
3 teaspoons dried oregano
freshly ground black pepper

Dressing
2 tablespoons lemon juice
2 egg yolks
2 anchovy fillets, finely chopped
2 tablespoons chopped small, black
    Niçoise olives

Salad
250 g/9 oz cherry tomatoes, blanched
    and peeled
200 g/7 oz green beans, blanched
12 small new potatoes, cooked, peeled
    and cut in half
white leaves from 1 head of celery,
    finely chopped
^{1}/$_4$ bunch of flat leaf parsley, leaves
    picked and chopped

1 Heat 1 tablespoon of the olive oil in a large heavy-based frying pan, add the garlic and anchovies and cook until the anchovies have melted. Season the fish with the oregano and pepper, add to the pan, reduce heat to very low and seal on both sides until just white. Add the remaining olive oil so that the fish is covered, and leave to poach in the oil for 30 minutes: the temperature of the oil should never be too hot (you should be able to put your finger in and count to three). After 30 minutes, the fish should still look a little undercooked. Remove and leave to cool, reserving the oil.

2 To make the dressing, combine the lemon juice with the egg yolks in a food processor and blend until thick. Keeping the motor running, gradually drizzle in the reserved olive oil and process until all the oil is absorbed and you have a mayonnaise consistency. Add the anchovies and olives and season with salt and pepper.

3 To make the salad, combine the cherry tomatoes, beans and potatoes and toss with a few tablespoons of the dressing. Arrange on serving plates. Carefully slice the kingfish fillet and evenly divide between the plates. Drizzle with a little extra dressing, sprinkle over the celery and parsley and serve.

Ben O'Donoghue

Blackened shark with shiso cress salad

This recipe is cooked in many famous Asian restaurants, and they charge the earth for it. Now you can do it at home! You can also marinate and cook chicken in the same way. If you're feeling tricky, try and cook some game with the miso marinade.

SERVES 4

Miso marinade
500 ml/18 fl oz white miso
250 ml/9 fl oz mirin
275 g/9 ³/4 oz caster sugar

4 x 200 g/7 oz shark fillets

Salad
1 punnet shiso cress*
¹/4 bunch of coriander
4 spring onions, white part only, finely sliced
1 frisée, white part only
1 teaspoon sesame oil
1 tablespoon lime juice
sea salt and freshly ground black pepper
1 teaspoon sesame seeds

1. To make the miso marinade, combine the miso with the mirin and the sugar in a glass bowl. Place the bowl over a saucepan of simmering water and cook for 1 hour or until the sugar is completely dissolved. Allow the miso marinade to cool. Reserve a small amount to dress the salad and drizzle over dish.

2. Place the shark fillets in a shallow ceramic dish and pour over the miso marinade. Marinate for 24 hours, turning several times.

3. To make the salad, combine the shiso cress, coriander, spring onions and frisée in a large bowl, dress with the sesame oil and lime juice and season with salt and pepper. Drizzle over some of the reserved miso marinade and sprinkle over the sesame seeds.

4. Preheat the grill to high. Place the shark fillets on a greaseproof paper-lined tray and spoon over some marinade. Cook under the grill for 8 minutes or until cooked. The top of the fish will caramelise slightly and should be black in parts. The fish is cooked once it starts to flake when pressed with a finger.

5. Place on plates next to a bed of salad. Drizzle some of the remaining marinade around the plate and serve.

* Shiso cress is an Asian herb with a cumin-like flavour. If unavailable, substitute with fresh mint.

Pot roast veal rump with roast vegetables

Roast veal is wonderful comfort food and this version is particularly good when the family comes for lunch or dinner.

SERVES 4–6

6 tablespoons olive oil
1.4 kg/3 lb boneless veal rump
100 ml/3½ fl oz Marsala
75 ml/2½ fl oz chicken stock
4 shallots (eschalots), peeled and cut in half
8 garlic cloves, peeled
16 baby new potatoes
2 carrots, peeled and cut diagonally into
    1.5 cm/¾ in slices
1 turnip, peeled and cut into wedges
fresh bay leaves, to garnish

1. Preheat the oven to 150°C/300°F/Gas Mark 2.

2. Heat 5 tablespoons of the olive oil in a large heavy-based flameproof casserole dish over high heat and seal the veal on all sides. Pour off any excess oil, return to the heat and deglaze with the Marsala.

3. Add the chicken stock and cover. Place in the oven for 1 hour, basting the meat with the juices every 15 minutes. Remove the veal, cover with foil and set aside to rest. Pour out the juices and reserve.

4. Increase oven temperature to 220°C/425°F/Gas Mark 7.

5. Wipe out the casserole dish with paper towel, place over a medium heat and drizzle in the remaining olive oil. Add the shallots, garlic, potatoes, carrots and turnip and colour slightly. Return the casserole dish to the oven, uncovered, and roast for 25 minutes or until cooked. Remove the vegetables, return the reserved juices to the pan and allow to reduce over medium heat for 2 minutes.

6. Return the veal to the casserole dish and put in the oven for 5 minutes. Then carve into thin slices and arrange on a platter surrounded by vegetables, garnished with bay leaves and any remaining roasting juices to serve.

Curtis Stone

Pears poached in sparkling shiraz with Parmigiano-Reggiano

A sophisticated, modern twist on an old classic.

SERVES 4

*4 Beurre Bosc pears, peeled with stems
    attached*
750 ml/1 bottle sparkling shiraz
375 ml/13^1/$_2$ fl oz port
50 g/2 oz caster sugar
1 cinnamon stick
1 vanilla bean, split lengthways
12 thin slices Parmigiano-Reggiano
*shaved Parmigiano-Reggiano,
    to serve (optional)*

1. Remove the core from the base of each pear using a melon baller, keeping the pear intact.

2. Place the sparkling shiraz, port, caster sugar, cinnamon and vanilla bean in a large saucepan and stir over a low heat to dissolve the sugar. Add the pears, bring to a simmer and cook for 50 minutes or until tender. Remove the pears, reserving the liquid, and slice a small portion from the bottom of each one to ensure they sit flat.

3. Place each pear on a serving plate. Cut each pear into three pieces at an angle (see image, left), arrange cheese slices between each piece.

4. Place 250 ml/9 fl oz of the reserved liquid in a small saucepan and bring to the boil. Reduce to a syrup. Drizzle the syrup around each plate and a small amount over the pears. Garnish the plate with extra Parmigiano-Reggiano shavings and serve.

Raspberry soufflé

The soufflé is one of the trickiest desserts to make because its success depends on so many factors. This recipe is pretty foolproof and looks and tastes fantasic — one to pull out when you need to impress.

SERVES 8

Base
500 ml/18 fl oz fruit puree
   (I love raspberry)
125 g/4$\frac{1}{2}$ oz caster sugar
4 teaspoons cornflour
water

Soufflé mix
10 egg whites
pinch of salt
100 g/3$\frac{1}{2}$ oz caster sugar
200 g/7 oz butter, softened, enough to
   grease the moulds
100 g/3$\frac{1}{2}$ oz caster sugar,
   enough to coat the moulds
icing sugar, for dusting
raspberries, to serve

1. To make the base, place the fruit puree and sugar in a saucepan over a medium heat. Stir to dissolve the sugar and bring to the boil. Mix the cornflour with just enough water to make a smooth paste. Once the fruit puree reaches boiling point, reduce the heat to low and whisk the cornflour paste into the fruit puree a little at a time. Whisk for 1 minute and do not allow mixture to boil again. Remove from the heat and set aside. Chill to cool completely.

2. Preheat the oven to 180°C/350°F/Gas Mark 4.

3. Place the egg whites into a very clean, very large mixing bowl, add the salt and beat at high speed until soft peaks form. Add the sugar, a little at a time, and beat until stiff peaks form. Do not over whisk or the egg whites will break down and be unable to hold the air required to lift the soufflé.

4. Place the fruit puree base into a very large bowl and whisk until smooth. Add a little of the egg white mixture and stir in to loosen the consistency. Gently fold in the remaining egg white.

continued opposite...

5. Brush the bases of 6 x 1-cup capacity ramekins with the softened butter, then, using upward strokes (this is very important), brush the sides. Chill in the refrigerator until set, and then repeat. Sprinkle in a little of the caster sugar, turning the ramekins to coat the base and sides. To fill the moulds, use a palette knife to spread the soufflé mixture around the sides while holding the ramekin at a 45-degree angle. Fill the middle and smooth the top, without allowing any mixture to stick to the rim or run over the sides.

6. Place in the oven and bake for 12–14 minutes or until golden and well risen. Serve immediately dusted with icing sugar, and with fresh raspberries on the side, if you like.

Ben O'Donoghue

Fremantle and Rottnest Island

Fremantle and Rottnest Island

Working harbour, holiday isle

Fremantle, or Freo as it is known to the locals, is a historic port and fishing boat harbour town on the west coast of Australia. And Rottnest, or Rotto, is a holiday island just 20 minutes west by ferry.

The reason we were here is that Ben used to live in Freo and it was on Rotto that he had his life-changing epiphany, but more about that later.

Many Italian and Greek descendents, first generation Australians, still earn their living from fishing out of the Fremantle Boat Harbour, and Jim Mendolia is one of them.

Jim tells the story of when his parents arrived here by ship in the 1950s, they couldn't believe their eyes when they saw school after school of sardines swarming around the ship as it entered Fremantle Harbour. Back in Sicily, sardines are much sought after, just as they are in Spain, Portugal and Greece. But back then, sardines were used as bait or sold to the recently arrived Italians who knew their true flavour and worth.

It's the warm Leeuwin Current that flows down the West Australian coast that's the reason why lobsters, sardines and most sea life flourish here.

Most of Jim's family went into fishing, even though their father tried to discourage them: Jim's brothers, Carmelo and Aldo, catch lobster in the rich fishing grounds just out of Fremantle.

In the early days, fishing for sardines was done in a traditional manner which meant once they spotted the school they used to row like crazy and try and encircle the school with the net. Nowadays they use a similar method, except they don't row after the schools, they motor after them. It must have been hard work because we only had to help pull in one net by hand and we were really stuffed. It's hard work.

Tastes change and nowadays Jim has a very successful business catching and selling filleted marinated and smoked local sardines right across the country. Jim got the idea to fillet them after seeing a herring-filleting machine in Europe. A few modifications, and away it went here in Freo. Turning out filleted sardines by the thousands. Jim now has three boats fishing.

Rottnest is a holiday island just 30 minutes off Fremantle. Luke Longley, the champion Australian basketballer who played alongside Michael Jordan with the Chicago Bulls and has three championship rings to prove it, picked us up and off we went. On the way out we passed a fleet of yachts racing with the wind behind them. Sydney might have the harbour, but Western Australia remains an ocean-sailing mecca.

The reason we were going to Rotto was because that was where Ben had his life-changing flash of inspiration. Bender had enrolled in teachers' training college, but in the summer holidays prior to starting his studies he took a job as a kitchen-hand on Rottnest. It was here that it hit him like a brick: what a great life it would be to be able to work at night (in a kitchen) and surf all day (his real love and joy). The rest, as they say, is history. Although it's pretty certain that working 15 hours a day running a top London restaurant doesn't leave much time for surfing! Still, Bender's involvement in TV cooking programmes and cookbooks is probably teaching of a kind...

Over on Rotto there are no cars, just pushbikes. So getting about is fun and exercise. We took a tandem bike and were able to carry our surfboards with us. We wandered down to one of the many beautiful bays and we all went snorkeling for western rock lobsters. In season, there are literally thousands of them under almost every rock ledge. Now we're OK at snorkelling, but Luke is a pro. He's a deft hand with the lasso that he slips neatly over the lobsters' bodies and uses to slide them out. Within a very short period of time we had dinner — fit for a king.

Ross Cameliri is another son of an Italian immigrant who's been unable to resist the call of the sea. His quarry is the octopus (or occi as the locals call it), which Aussies also once considered to be fit only for bait. Today, thanks to Ross and others, it's now seen as the gourmet dish it is in Spain and Italy and Greece and Croatia and so on.

Ross has over 8000 pots laid out in the placid waters just off Fremantle. None of them are set with baits. The occi just see the pots and think they'd make lovely homes. Ross and his workers then come along and pull the pots. Simple. They use a GPS these days to find them. Ross and his boys pull around 1200 pots on lines each day. Back at his modest factory they process the octopus simply, either by smoking it or pickling it. They also sell it fresh or frozen, mostly to restaurants and gourmet food stores.

Perhaps the reason the octopus tastes so wonderful here is that their diet is of lobster and scallop and crab. You can almost taste them in their flesh. The best advice Ross can give on cooking occi is not to cook them on the day you catch them. Leave them or freeze them to allow the high proportion of fluid to break down.

Little Creatures is a boutique brewery right on the Freo fishing boat harbour. The reason we went to investigate their produce is because they use the same theory as we do in our cooking. That is, fresh ingredients, craftsmanship, flair and a recipe. No really, that's why we visited...

Anyway, the name 'Little Creatures' is a reference to the tiny organisms that come to life and turn raw ingredients into beer. This beer's all natural and not pasteurised because the hops act as a natural preserving agent — and because they believe that pasteurising dulls the flavour. The little creatures are touchy too, so care must be taken not to put them under any stress.

Mussels steamed in beer and thyme

Fresh mussels cooked quickly — simply brilliant. Serve with a cold beer and tuck in.

1 tablespoon olive oil
4 kg/8 lb 13 oz mussels, bearded
*   and scrubbed*
4 shallots (eschalots), finely chopped
2 garlic cloves, crushed
2 sprigs of thyme
3 bay leaves
200 ml/7 fl oz beer
2 tablespoons finely chopped flat
*   leaf parsley*
75 g/2 ¾ oz butter, chopped into dice
Extra finely chopped flat leaf parsley,
*   for garnish*

1. Heat a large saucepan over a high heat until very hot. Add the oil, mussels, shallots, garlic, thyme and bay leaves and toss quickly. Add the beer, cover, and cook for 2–3 minutes or until the mussels begin to open. Add the parsley and toss through.

2. Heat a medium saucepan over a high heat. Strain the liquid from the mussels into the saucepan. Return the mussels, discarding any that have not opened, to the large saucepan, cover, and keep warm. Bring the mussel liquid to the boil for 1 minute, add the butter and whisk until the butter has melted.

3. Place the mussels in a large serving bowl, pour over the butter sauce, sprinkle over parsley, and serve immediately.

Curtis Stone

Spicy coconut mussel broth

This is an excellent winter warmer. Eat the mussels, then drink the spicy liquor and enjoy. Don't over-season with fish sauce until you've opened the mussels as the broth could become too salty.

SERVES 4

1 L/1³/₄ pints chicken stock

2 x 400 ml/14¹/₄ fl oz cans coconut milk

5 kaffir lime leaves

4 sticks lemon grass, white part
    only, bruised

5 cm/2 in piece of ginger, sliced

5 cm/2 in piece of galangal, sliced

fish sauce, to taste

2 teaspoons vegetable oil

1 bunch of coriander with roots, chopped,
    leaves reserved for garnish

2 kg/4¹/₂ lb black mussels, scrubbed and
    debearded

2 red chillies, finely sliced

1. To make the broth, combine the stock, coconut milk, lime leaves, lemon grass, ginger and galangal in a large saucepan over medium to high heat and bring to the boil. Reduce the heat slightly and simmer until reduced by half. Season with the fish sauce and keep warm.

2. Heat the vegetable oil in a large heavy-based saucepan and sauté the chopped coriander stalks and roots, reserving the leaves for the garnish, for 1 minute. Add the mussels and immediately pour in the broth. Cover with a tight-fitting lid and bring to the boil. Cook, shaking the pan from time to time, for 5 minutes or so until the mussels open. Discard any mussels that haven't opened.

3. Sprinkle over the coriander leaves and chilli and serve immediately.

Ben O'Donoghue

Sardine sandwich

People often ask what chefs eat for dinner. Well, here it is: quick, simple and very tasty.

SERVES 4

Tapenade
150 g/5½ oz pitted kalamata olives
2 teaspoons baby capers (if salted, soak in
   cold water for 30 minutes and
   rinse well)
1½ tablespoons extra virgin olive oil
1 tablespoon lemon juice
1 garlic clove, chopped
1 tablespoon sherry vinegar

8 slices ciabatta bread or similar Italian-style
   crusty bread
olive oil, for brushing
8 small sardines, already filleted
   or butterflied
50 g/2 oz mixed baby herbs

1. To make the tapenade, place the olives, capers, olive oil, lemon juice, garlic and sherry vinegar in a food processor and process until smooth.

2. Brush the bread slices with the olive oil. Heat a chargrill plate until hot. Cook the bread for 3–4 minutes on each side or until lightly charred.

3. Reheat the chargrill plate over high heat until very hot. Brush with a little olive oil and cook the sardines, skin-side down, for 1 minute. Turn and cook for a further 30 seconds.

4. Place 2 slices of bread on each serving plate and drizzle a little tapenade over each slice. Arrange the sardines to one side of the bread. Place a dollop of tapenade on each plate, garnish with the herbs and serve.

Curtis Stone

Octopus salad with tomato, lime and chilli

I reckon that octopus is often misused. If you find that when you cook it you spend half your time bashing it, then look no further than this recipe. It requires temperature-resistant hands but the burns are worth every skin graft!

SERVES 4

1 large octopus, weighing about
    1.5 kg/3 lb 5 oz
2 carrots, finely chopped
1 onion, finely chopped
3 garlic cloves, peeled
1 teaspoon black peppercorns
1/4 bunch parsley, chopped
1 bay leaf
salt
large square of muslin

Dressing
500 g/1 lb 2 oz ripe tomatoes, peeled,
    seeded and chopped
4 red chillies, grilled, peeled, deseeded
    and chopped
juice and finely grated zest of 3 limes
250 ml/9 fl oz extra virgin olive oil
sea salt and freshly ground black pepper

1 iceberg lettuce, washed and finely sliced
lime juice and olive oil, for dressing
1/4 bunch of coriander, leaves picked and
    chopped

1. Remove the eyes and beak from the octopus and wash thoroughly. Place in a large saucepan with the carrots, onion, garlic, peppercorns, parsley and bay leaf. Cover with cold water and season with salt. Bring to the boil and simmer for about 2 hours or until the octopus is very tender.

2. Wearing rubber gloves, remove the octopus from the pan and place on muslin. Roll the octopus up into a ball so that all the legs fold inwards, then twist the muslin into a very tight ball and tie tightly with string. Place in a large bowl and refrigerate until cold. The octopus will set firm. The best results are after chilling for 24 hours.

3. To make the dressing, combine the tomatoes, chillies, lime juice and zest and olive oil in a bowl and season with salt and pepper.

4. Dress the lettuce with a squeeze of lime juice and some olive oil (or some of the liquid from the tomato dressing), and arrange it in a mound on a serving plate. Using a sharp knife, slice across the octopus and arrange the slices on the lettuce. Dress liberally with the tomato dressing and finish with the coriander.

Ben O'Donoghue

Spaghetti con la sardi

This is a classic and one of my all-time favourite pasta recipes; I always have it when I go to Italy. There is just something so complete about the sweet and sour flavours of the currants and lemon-rich oiliness of the sardine.

SERVES 4

4 tablespoons olive oil
1 large red onion, finely chopped
2 fennel bulbs, finely chopped, tops reserved
2 garlic cloves, crushed
2 tablespoons pine nuts
2 tablespoons currants, soaked in dry
 Marsala for 20 minutes, drained
sea salt and freshly ground black pepper
500 g/1 lb 2 oz spaghetti
16 sardine fillets
80 ml/2 ³/₄ fl oz dry white wine
2 tablespoons finely chopped flat
 leaf parsley
finely grated zest of 1 lemon

1. Gently heat 2 tablespoons of the olive oil in a large, deep heavy-based frying pan. Add the onion and fennel and cook over a low heat until the vegetables are golden and soft. Add the garlic, pine nuts and currants, season with the salt and pepper and remove from the heat.

2. Cook the spaghetti in a large pot of boiling salted water until *al dente*. Drain.

3. Reheat the pan with the vegetables over a medium heat and place the sardine fillets on top. Drizzle with the remaining olive oil, add the white wine, cover, and reduce the heat to low. Cook for about 5 minutes or until the sardines are just cooked through.

4. Add the spaghetti to the sardines, gently turning the pasta through the fish and sauce to coat. Divide between warmed serving plates and sprinkle over the reserved fennel tops, parsley and lemon zest and serve.

Ben O'Donoghue

Lobster with free-range chicken and shellfish foam

My version of a Surf and Turf. The combination of flavours here are incredible, but be warned that there is a bit to do in this recipe.

SERVES 4

2 x 700 g/1¹/₂ lb (shell-on weight) rock lobsters
1 carrot, roughly chopped
1 onion, roughly chopped
1 celery stick, roughly chopped
50 g/2 oz sugar
50 g/2 oz butter
pinch of salt
12 chicken oysters
12 cherry tomatoes, on the vine
2 tablespoons olive oil
12 thin slices pancetta
200 g/7 oz snow peas (mange tout)
sea salt and freshly ground black pepper
100 ml/3¹/₂ fl oz shellfish foam (see Sea urchins with fennel puree and shellfish foam on page 73)

1. Place the lobsters in the freezer for 2 hours or until they stop moving.

2. Preheat the oven to 200°C/400°F/Gas Mark 6.

3. Place the carrot, onion and celery in a large saucepan of cold water and bring to the boil. Turn off the heat and allow to sit for 1 minute. Add the lobsters and leave in the hot water for 3–4 minutes. Remove the lobster meat from the shell and reserve the meat and legs.

4. Place the sugar in a hot saucepan and allow to caramelise, watching carefully. Once golden brown, stir in the butter and salt. Reduce heat to low, add the chicken oysters and cook for 3–4 minutes, turning occasionally.

5. Place the lobster meat and legs and the cherry tomatoes in a small non-stick baking tray and drizzle with the olive oil. Place in the oven for 3–4 minutes.

6. Lay the slices of pancetta on greaseproof paper and place under a hot grill until crispy.

continued opposite…

Curtis Stone

7 Blanch the snow peas in boiling water for 1 minute and season with the salt and pepper.

8 Warm the shellfish foam in a saucepan over a low heat, then remove and froth with a hand blender.

9 On warmed serving plates, arrange the lobster, slices of pancetta, chicken oysters, snow peas and lobster legs. Drizzle with a little caramel, spoon over the shellfish foam and serve.

Dhufish with white bean puree and baby octopus

Here is a protein-packed recipe. I love mixing seafood and beans because it gives good body to the dish.

SERVES 4

2 tablespoons olive oil

4 shallots (eschalots), finely sliced

1 teaspoon finely chopped rosemary leaves

10 sage leaves, finely chopped

2 garlic cloves, crushed

300 g/11 oz cannelloni beans, soaked
  overnight

75 ml/^{1}/$_3$ cup white wine

500 ml/18 fl oz chicken stock

2^1/$_2$ tablespoons extra virgin olive oil

2 tablespoons finely chopped flat leaf parsley

4 x 200 g/7 oz dhufish fillets, skin on

300 g/11 oz baby octopus, cleaned and
  quartered

3 tablespoons sherry vinegar

1. Heat 1 tablespoon of the olive oil in a large, heavy-based frying pan over medium heat, add the shallots, rosemary, sage and garlic and sauté until soft. Add the beans, deglaze with the white wine and reduce for 2 minutes. Add the chicken stock and simmer for 20 minutes or until the beans are tender. Remove 75 g/2^3/$_4$ oz of the beans and reserve for the garnish. Continue cooking the beans for a further 15 minutes or until they begin to fall apart. Strain and place the beans in a food processor and process until smooth. Pour the extra virgin olive oil in through the funnel while the motor is still running. Add 1 tablespoon of the parsley, return to the pan and keep warm over a very low heat.

2. Heat a non-stick frying pan over medium heat and cook the fish, skin-side down, for 2 minutes. Turn and cook for a further 2 minutes.

3. Heat the remaining 1 tablespoon of olive oil in a separate frying pan over high heat and cook the octopus for 30 seconds. Add the remaining 1 tablespoon of parsley and deglaze the pan with the sherry vinegar.

4. Place 2–3 spoonfuls of the white bean puree in the centre of each serving plate, top with the fish and garnish the outside of the plate with the reserved beans and the octopus. Drizzle over the juices from the pan and serve.

Curtis Stone

Barbecued leg of lamb with fattoush

Fattoush is a simple salad made from stale or dried bread, chopped herbs and bulghur wheat, which is kind of like cous cous. Coupled with beautiful barbecued lamb you've got the perfect Sunday lunch.

SERVES 4–6

Marinade

3 garlic cloves, finely chopped
2 tablespoons coriander seeds, crushed
juice of 2 lemons
100 ml/3^1/2 fl oz olive oil
3 teaspoons smoked paprika
1.8 kg/3 lb 15^1/2 oz leg of lamb,
    boned and butterflied

Fattoush

2 rounds of Lebanese bread
1 tablespoon olive oil
250 g/9 oz bulghur wheat
1 bunch of flat leaf parsley, leaves
    picked and chopped
1 bunch of mint, leaves picked and roughly
    chopped
1 bunch of coriander, leaves picked and
    chopped
250 g/9 oz cherry tomatoes, roughly chopped

Dressing

2 garlic cloves
100 ml/3^1/2 fl oz olive oil
3 tablespoons lemon juice
2 teaspoons ground sumac*
sea salt and freshly ground black pepper

*Sumac is a Middle Eastern spice that is sold ground or in dried berry form.

1. To make the marinade, combine the garlic, coriander seeds, lemon juice, olive oil and paprika in a mixing bowl.

2. Place the lamb in a large ceramic dish and rub the marinade all over. Cover and refrigerate for 3–4 hours or overnight.

3. Preheat a covered barbecue to medium low. Cook the lamb for 40 minutes with the lid on, turning twice. The lamb will be medium. Remove and rest for 20 minutes.

4. Preheat the oven to 200°C/400°F/Gas Mark 6.

5. To make the fattoush, brush the bread with the olive oil and bake in the oven for 5 minutes or until crisp. Break up the bread into large bite-sized pieces. Place the bulghur in a heatproof bowl and cover with boiling water. Stand for 10 minutes. Drain and squeeze out the excess water. Combine with parsley, mint, coriander, cherry tomatoes and the broken-up flat bread.

6. To make the dressing, pound the garlic in a mortar and add the olive oil, lemon juice, sumac and season with salt and pepper. Toss through the fattoush.

7. Slice the lamb, arrange on a platter, pour over the meat juices and serve with the fattoush.

Caramelised pineapple and brioche

If you're wanting a rich, sticky desert, then look no further!

SERVES 4

1 pineapple, trimmed
450 g/1 lb loaf brioche
200 g/7 oz caster sugar
50 g/2 oz butter, diced
1 cinnamon stick
1 vanilla bean, split lengthways
100 ml/3^1/2 fl oz Malibu rum
100 ml/3^1/2 fl oz pineapple juice
75 ml/2^1/2 fl oz cream
4 scoops of cinnamon ice-cream*

1. Cut the pineapple into four 2 cm/^{3}/4 in slices. Remove the core, then trim the edges and remove the eyes to make neatly edged discs.

2. Cut the brioche into four 2 cm/^{3}/4in thick slices, then into discs the same size as the pineapple.

3. Heat a large, non-stick frying pan over a medium heat, add the sugar and cook for 10 minutes or until the sugar has melted and turned a caramel colour. As the sugar will begin melting from the outside of the pan, make sure you shake the pan to ensure it doesn't burn. Do not stir the sugar as it will crystallise. Add the butter, cinnamon and vanilla bean. Once the butter has melted, stir in the Malibu and pineapple juice.

4. Place the pineapple discs in the syrup and cook for 5 minutes on each side. Set aside.

5. Add the cream to the syrup and place the brioche slices in the syrup and cook for 1 minute on each side. Transfer the cooked brioche slices to serving plates, top with the pineapple and a scoop of cinnamon ice-cream. Drizzle the outside of each plate with the remaining syrup and serve.

*If cinnamon ice-cream is unavailable, add ground cinnamon to softened vanilla ice-cream, stir until combined and return to the freezer.

Beer parfait with salted peanut caramel

Beer and salted peanuts — what a perfect combination! Actually so is beer and spicy sausage but you would have to be mad to make ice-cream out of that ... The salty peanut caramel can be set or used as a sauce. It will keep for up to two weeks in the freezer.

SERVES 4–6

Pâte bombe
160 g/5$\frac{1}{2}$ oz caster sugar

water

8 egg yolks

Parfait
1 gelatine leaf

250 ml/9 fl oz strong beer with flavour,
    such as Little Creature's Pale Ale or
    Guiness

100 ml/3$\frac{1}{2}$ fl oz pouring cream, whipped

Peanut caramel
100 g/3$\frac{1}{2}$ oz sugar

water

3 tablespoons pouring cream

40 g/1$\frac{1}{2}$ oz crushed salted peeled peanuts
    (groundnuts)

pinch of salt

1 To make the pâte bombe, make a paste by combining the sugar with a little water in a saucepan. Slowly bring to the boil and cook until the hard ball stage is reached (you will need a sugar thermometer). Whisk the egg yolks in a mixer until light and fluffy, then pour in the sugar syrup and whisk until cold, approximately 5–10 minutes. This mixture will keep for a day.

2 To make the parfait, soak the gelatine in water until soft. Squeeze dry and melt in the microwave on low or warm in a bowl over a simmering saucepan of water. Add to the beer and whisk to combine. Cover with cling wrap and refrigerate until just starting to set, about 10 minutes. Fold the whipped cream into the set beer. Then fold the pâte bombe into the mixture. Line an 800-ml/1$\frac{1}{2}$-pint capacity mould with several layers of cling wrap and fill with the parfait mixture. Place in the freezer to set.

continued opposite...

3. To make the peanut caramel, combine the sugar and a little water in a saucepan, mix to a paste and cook to a golden caramel. Whisk in the cream and peanuts and reduce on a rapid boil for 2 to 3 minutes. Add the salt and pour onto greaseproof paper. Cover with another sheet of greaseproof paper and roll out thinly. Cut into shapes and allow to cool completely so that it becomes hard. (Or, alternatively, use as a hot sauce; it's easier.) Serve the parfait with the peanut caramel and some commerically made chocolate sauce.

Ben O'Donoghue

Kakadu

Kakadu

Ancient land, modern world

Kakadu is a World Heritage-listed national park in the north of Australia, about three hours' drive south-east of Darwin. It's a tropical, wetland paradise. The park is managed in consultation between the traditional owners (Australian indigenous people) and the Federal Government. It is a unique example of cooperation and understanding and it shows in the park.

We waited by the river crossing between Arnham Land and Kakadu for our lift. Eventually, a battered 'Toyota troopie' splashed its way across the river and stopped. Thankfully it was our lift; 19-year-old daughter of traditional owner Jonathon Nadji, Natasha. Tash's grandfather, Bill Neidjie is well known as a great leader and also as a poet, author of *Gagudju Man* — that really sums up the relationship between these people and the land.

Tash's Dreaming place, or Mushroom Rock as she calls it, is her special place, her place of solitude. A weird, mushroom-shaped natural rock structure that appears to defy gravity, it has remarkable centuries-old paintings on the underside. On this rock there was also an indented depression, which is where Tash's relatives have been coming to pound seeds for tens of thousands of years.

Tash introduced us to her father, Jonathon, at Ubirr Rock. The rock paintings at Ubirr are in a huge overhang of a rock-like open cave and the art is found here in profusion. Even though there's a painting of a man in white with his hands in his pocket, and another white figure with a pipe (probably depictions of early European explorers), some of these paintings have been carbon-dated back more than 50,000 years. In this region, Jonathon explains, the paintings are mostly of the food that these peoples have hunted and eaten for thousands upon thousands of years. Tortoises and geese are there, but the most common is barramundi, one of the local and most prized fish in the region. Prized right around Australia too. These barramundi paintings, so Jonathon tells us, are like textbooks for children. They show the skeleton, the fat areas, the flesh and the stomach.

Having established our love of barra (barramundi), Jonathon suggested we go catch some. Barra is a local type of perch. Again, being there with Tash and her family meant that we were taken

to yet more places where the normal visitor does not get the chance to visit, such as the Jabiluka billabong, a beautiful, blue stretch of water with waterlilies floating near the edge. It looked so peaceful. But don't think about swimming, there are crocodiles in there, too. Big ones.

We saw a couple of croc nests (they lay their eggs on shore and cover them with mounds of leaves and soil which holds in the warmth of the daily sun), but we didn't see the crocs themselves.

Not long after, Bender had a bite, then another, then another. It was like the dream you have, almost every cast catches a fish. Bender is a natural fisherman, but eventually Curtis hooked one too.

The locals cook their fish very simply. They peel the pliable bark from the local weeping paperbark tree (*Melaleuca*) and they wrap it around the fish much as we would use aluminium foil so that the fish cook in their own steam. Simple and delicious.

Tash and some of her brothers took us hunting a local delicacy, Magpie Geese. This meant going into the wetlands. The goose was butterflied and laid onto the pandanas palm nut coals where it gently sizzled. There was a wonderfully nutty, smoky flavour to the goose meat. It was delicious.

It was such a privilege to have spent this time with these locals and to experience their respect for and sense of belonging with the land. Their sense of the land is developed to such an extent that they can see food everywhere. While we, on most occasions, can't see the forest for the trees.

Rillette of goose with chardonnay jelly

Everybody talks about food and wine matching. Well in this recipe I am taking it one step further. By turning a wine into a jelly you are getting the best of both worlds on your plate.

SERVES 4–6

Chardonnay jelly

750 ml/1 bottle chardonnay
3 tablespoons caster sugar
3¹/₂ leaves of gelatine

Rillette

4 goose legs
125 g/4¹/₂ oz rock salt
4 garlic cloves, crushed
2 sprigs of thyme
8 bay leaves
1 kg/2 lb 4 oz goose fat
15 g/¹/₂ oz green peppercorns
extra virgin olive oil, to drizzle
8 slices of crusty bread
10 cornichons (small gherkins),
    sliced lengthways

① Combine 1¹/₂ cups of the chardonnay with the caster sugar in a saucepan. Bring to the boil and reduce by half. Add the remaining 1¹/₂ cups of chardonnay, bring to the boil and reduce by a third.

② Soften the gelatine in cold water. Squeeze out the gelatine leaves and slowly stir into the hot chardonnay syrup until dissolved. When cooled slightly, pour into a plastic container, cover, and allow to set in the refrigerator for approximately 3 hours.

③ Place the goose legs in a large container. Cover with the rock salt, garlic, thyme and bay leaves and marinate in the refrigerator for 12–24 hours.

④ Preheat the oven to 120°C/250°F/Gas Mark ¹/₂.

⑤ To make the confit, wash the excess salt off the goose legs. Place them in a large heavy-based flameproof casserole dish and cover with the goose fat. Bring to just below boiling point, remove from the heat and cover. Transfer to the oven and cook for 3 hours or until the meat falls off the bone.

continued opposite...

Note: Rillettes will keep refrigerated for 4–6 weeks.

Curtis Stone

6. While still warm, remove the meat from the goose legs, discarding the bones and skin, and mix with the peppercorns. Stir briskly with a fork to break down the meat. Add 150 g/5½ oz of the goose fat in which the legs were cooked and mix in well. Pack the rillette meat firmly into ½-cup ramekins. Refrigerate until ready to serve.

7. Drizzle a little of the extra virgin olive oil over the bread and chargrill until golden brown.

8. Break the chardonnay jelly into pieces the size of small dice.

9. Serve the rillettes with the cornichons, pieces of chardonnay jelly, chargrilled bread and a good drizzle of the extra virgin olive oil.

Curtis Stone

Vietnamese crispy pancakes

I discovered these pancakes in London: in Hackney, where I live, there are many Vietnamese restaurants that serve them. They are a great dish to share.

SERVES 4

Filling

2 teaspoons sesame oil

200 g/7oz firm tofu, drained and diced

1 teaspoon finely grated ginger

2 garlic cloves, crushed

1 can bamboo shoots, rinsed

1 bunch of spring onions, chopped

1 white onion, thinly sliced

salt

150 g/5 oz shaved fresh coconut

Batter

350 g/12 oz rice flour

$^1/_2$ teaspoon ground turmeric

pinch of salt

1 teaspoon sugar

750 ml/1 pint 7 fl oz coconut milk

2 teaspoons sunflower oil, plus extra to
    grease pan

250ml/9fl oz water, plus a little more if
    required to make batter smooth

Garnish

1 teaspoon sesame seeds

8 iceberg lettuce leaves

$^1/_2$ bunch of Thai basil, leaves picked

$^1/_2$ bunch of Vietnamese mint, leaves picked

2 limes, quartered

① To make the filling, heat the sesame oil in a wok and stir-fry the tofu until golden. Set aside. Stir-fry the ginger, garlic, bamboo shoots, spring onions and onion for 2–3 minutes or until just tender. Season with salt and add the shaved coconut and stir to combine. Remove from the heat, set aside and keep warm.

② To make the batter, sift the rice flour, turmeric, salt and sugar into a mixing bowl. Stir in the coconut milk, sunflower oil and water until well combined and the batter is smooth with the consistency of pouring cream.

③ Heat a large, non-stick frying pan over a medium to high heat, and lightly grease with a little sunflower oil. Pour in enough batter to cover the pan and swirl around to make a thin crêpe. Cook on one side only for 3-5 minutes or until golden and crisp.

④ Make, fill and eat pancakes one at a time. Fill the crêpe and fold over, then transfer to a serving platter.

⑤ Serve the herbs and lettuce on a separate plate. Wrap portions of the crêpe and some herbs in the lettuce like san choy bau. Add a squeeze of lime. Then repeat until all the crêpe batter has been used.

Rice paper rolls with mud crab, rosella and mango

What I love most about these rice paper rolls are the freshness of the rosella and the sweetness of the crab. I remember as a kid living in Port Hedland eating fresh rosella, and screwing my face up at how sour they were. But like this, they're fantastic.

SERVES 4

12 x 17 cm/6 ³/₄ in square rice paper
    wrappers (get a few extra to allow
    for breakages)
1 bunch of mint, leaves picked
1 bunch of coriander, leaves picked
1 mango, cut into 1 cm/¹/₂ in strips
8–10 fresh rosella fruit petals, peeled
    and sliced*
250 g/9 oz cooked crabmeat, picked over
1 bunch of garlic chives

Dipping sauce
125 ml/4¹/₂ fl oz rice vinegar
50 g/2 oz caster sugar
2¹/₂ teaspoons fish sauce
¹/₂ small Lebanese cucumber, seeded
    and finely diced
¹/₂ small green mango, finely diced
1 teaspoon chopped mint
juice of 1 lime

1. Soak the rice paper wrappers, one at a time, in hot water for about 30 seconds until softened. Place on a clean tea towel and gently pat dry. Take care as the rice paper is fragile. Along the bottom edge of the rice paper, place a line of mint leaves, coriander, mango and rosella, and top with the crabmeat. Fold the bottom edge over the filling, and roll once, then fold in one side and roll once more. Fold in the other side and finish rolling. Secure with a garlic chive. Repeat this process for all the wrappers and filling.

2. To make the dipping sauce, bring the vinegar and sugar to the boil in a small saucepan. Allow to cool then stir in the remaining ingredients. Pour into small serving bowls.

3. Arrange the rice paper rolls on a serving platter and serve with the dipping sauce.

Rosella fruit petals may be substituted with sour fruits such as cranberries or green mango.

Salad of mud crab and ruby grapefruit with vinaigrette

In Australia we are so lucky to be able to get our hands on good quality crabs. Treat them very simply so you don't overshadow their beautiful sweet flavour. Here I just serve the crab meat with some grapefruit and a vinaigrette.

SERVES 4

Vinaigrette
2¹/₂ tablespoons tarragon vinegar
1 garlic clove, crushed
¹/₂ small shallot (eschalot), chopped
1 tablespoon extra virgin olive oil
2 tablespoons grape seed oil
2 teaspoons chopped chives
sea salt and freshly ground black pepper

300 g/11 oz picked cooked crabmeat
40 g/1¹/₂ oz picked watercress
3 ruby grapefruits, segmented
mixed baby herbs, to garnish

1. To make the vinaigrette, place the vinegar in a small bowl, add the garlic and shallot and whisk in the extra virgin olive oil and grape seed oil. Strain and discard the shallot and garlic. Stir in the chives and season with salt and pepper.

2. Combine 2 teaspoons of the vinaigrette with the crabmeat in a bowl.

3. Position a 5 cm/2 in round cutter on a serving plate. Place a quarter of the watercress inside the cutter. Gently pack a quarter of the crab mixture on top of the watercress. Arrange a quarter of the grapefruit segments on top to cover the crabmeat. Gently remove the cutter, forming a stack, and garnish with the baby herbs.

4. Drizzle a quarter of the remaining dressing around the outside of the plate. Repeat this process to make four stacks and serve.

Curtis Stone

Curried mud crab

The truly great cuisines of the world are complex in flavour, simple in practice and deeply satisfying. This is a dish inspired by chefs from the south coast of India.

SERVES 2

1 kg/2 lb 4 oz live mud crab

Paste
4 tablespoons coriander seeds
1½ tablespoons cumin seeds
1 tablespoon black peppercorns
1 white onion, chopped
50 g/2 oz desiccated coconut
1 large green chilli, chopped
1 tablespoon finely grated ginger
5 garlic cloves
150 ml/5½ fl oz white wine vinegar

1 tablespoon sunflower or canola oil
1 medium tomato, diced
10 curry leaves
10 g/½ oz fresh turmeric, peeled and
    finely grated
1 tablespoon chilli powder
sea salt
125 ml/4¼ fl oz water
250 ml/9 fl oz coconut milk

1. Place the crab in the freezer for 2 hours or until it stops moving. Remove the legs and crack with a rolling pin. Remove the top of the shell and clean out the insides with your fingers. Chop in half.

2. To make the paste, grind the coriander seeds, cumin seeds and peppercorns using a mortar and pestle or a spice grinder. Transfer to a food processor and add the onion, coconut, chilli, ginger, garlic and vinegar and blend to a paste.

3. Heat the oil in a large saucepan over a low heat, add the paste and sauté for 5–10 minutes or until fragrant. Add the tomato, curry leaves, turmeric, chilli powder and a pinch of salt and cook for 5 minutes. Add the crab and the water, increase heat to medium and bring to the boil. Reduce the heat to low and simmer for 10 minutes. Mix in the coconut milk and cook for 2–3 minutes. Serve with steamed rice.

Ben O'Donoghue

Barramundi baked in foil with zucchini, squash and Asian herbs

This can be assembled in 5 minutes and cooked in only 5 or 6, which means that you can make a lovely, healthy dinner from start to finish in about 15 minutes.

SERVES 4

3 zucchini (courgettes), cut into batons
5 yellow squash, cut into batons
1½ tablespoons light soy sauce
1 teaspoon sesame oil
1 tablespoon oyster sauce
1 tablespoon mirin
4 x 200 g/7 oz barramundi fillets
32 Thai basil leaves
24 sprigs of coriander
2 tablespoons vegetable oil
3 cm/1¼ in piece of ginger, julienned
4 shallots (eschalots), sliced
1 garlic clove, finely sliced
3 heads of baby bok choy, each cut into 4
1 teaspoon fish sauce

1. Preheat the oven to 220°C/425°F/Gas Mark 7.

2. Place a baking tray in the oven to preheat.

3. Divide the zucchini and squash between four pieces of foil 30 x 40 cm/12 x 16 in.

4. Combine the soy sauce, sesame oil, oyster sauce and mirin in a small bowl, whisk well, and drizzle over the zucchini and squash.

5. Place the barramundi and half of the basil and coriander on top of the zucchini and squash. Bring together the long sides of the foil and fold to enclose the fish parcel, ensuring that no steam can escape during cooking.

6. Place the parcels on the preheated baking tray and cook in the oven for 3–6 minutes, depending on the thickness of the fish fillets.

7. Heat the vegetable oil in a wok and swirl to coat. Add the ginger, shallots and garlic and cook for 30 seconds. Add the bok choy and toss for 1–2 minutes or until slightly wilted. Add the fish sauce and toss to coat. Place four pieces of bok choy on each serving plate.

continued opposite...

Curtis Stone

8 Open the parcels of fish. Remove and discard the herbs. Place the fish on top of the bok choy and place the zucchini and squash on top of the fish. Spoon the juices from the parcel around the outside of the plate. Finely chop the remaining Thai basil and coriander, sprinkle over the dish and serve.

Whole poached Asian barramundi

This was so good to cook! Not only did we catch the barra just hours before in a pristine billabong, but the joy with which it was devoured by Derrick, Tash's boyfriend, was quite a compliment. He even ate the eyes! This is a simple, clean recipe that will work with most white firm-fleshed fish.

SERVES 4

1.5 kg/3lb 5 oz whole barramundi, scaled, gutted and gills removed

Marinade

250 ml/9 fl oz Shaoxing rice wine*

Thick, 3 cm/1¼ in piece ginger, peeled and julienned

½ bunch of spring onions, sliced finely on the diagonal

150 ml/5½ fl oz light soy sauce

Sauce

2 teaspoons grated palm sugar

2 teaspoons light soy sauce

3 tablespoons yellow bean sauce or yellow bean paste

500 g/1 lb 2 oz wing beans, blanched

4 spring onions, chopped

½ teaspoon sesame oil

coriander leaves, to garnish

1. Score diagonal cuts across the thickest part of the barramundi, down to the bone, and place in a large shallow ceramic dish.

2. To make the marinade, combine the rice wine, ginger, spring onions and soy sauce and pour over the fish. Cover and refrigerate for 2–3 hours.

3. Place the fish in a large fish kettle or frying pan and pour over the marinade and enough water to cover. Bring to a simmer and cook gently for 20 minutes or until the largest spine can be pulled out easily. Transfer the fish, reserving the poaching liquid, to a serving platter.

4. To make the sauce, combine the palm sugar and a little of the poaching water in a wok over a medium heat. Add the soy sauce and yellow bean sauce and stir. Add the wing beans and 100 ml/3½ fl oz of the poaching liquid and bring to the boil for 2–3 minutes. Stir in the spring onions and sesame oil and pour over the fish. Garnish with coriander and serve.

Shaoxing rice wine is a traditional Chinese yellow rice wine. If unavailable, dry sherry or vermouth may be substituted.

Braised beef cheek with pommes puree

A basic rule of thumb when it comes to meat is: the more active a muscle, the more flavoursome the meat. The downside of the flavour, however, is the texture; an active piece of meat is usually tough. That's why beef cheeks are perfect to braise. You cook the meat until its tender and keep all of that lovely rich flavour.

SERVES 4

1 tablespoon olive oil

4 shallots (eschalots), quartered

2 bay leaves

1 sprig of thyme

2 carrots, cut into 2 cm/^{3}/$_4$ in pieces

2 celery sticks, cut into 2 cm/^{3}/$_4$ in pieces

1.4 kg/3 lb beef cheek, sinew removed, cut
     into 3 cm/1^1/$_4$ in pieces

1^1/$_2$ tablespoons tomato paste

6 garlic cloves, crushed

250 ml/9 fl oz red wine

350 ml/12^1/$_4$ fl oz veal stock

juice of ^{1}/$_2$ orange

500 g/1 lb 2 oz potatoes

salt and freshly ground black pepper,
     to taste

150 g/5^1/$_2$ oz butter, chopped into pieces

1. Heat the olive oil in a large heavy-based saucepan over a medium to high heat and add the shallots, bay leaves, thyme, carrots and celery and cook for 10 minutes or until lightly golden in colour.

2. Add the meat and cook for 5 minutes. Add the tomato paste and cook, stirring occasionally, for a further 5–10 minutes or until the ingredients start to stick to the base of the pan. Add the garlic and wine, reduce the heat and cook for 5 minutes or until reduced to a syrup. Add the stock, cover, and cook for 2 hours or until the beef is tender.

3. Stir through the orange juice.

4. To make the pommes puree, peel the potatoes and boil in water until tender. Drain and put through a potato ricer. Season and mix through the butter piece by piece, stirring constantly.

5. Spoon some pomme puree into a bowl and the braised beef cheek beside it.

Curtis Stone

Banana fritters

You just can't beat deep-fried food for flavour. Such a beautiful recipe, it's one of my wife's favourites, and she always talks about when she first ate it in Thailand.

SERVES 4

4 tablespoons cornflour, sifted
175 g/6^1/4 oz rice flour, sifted
1 tablespoon sesame seeds
4 tablespoons caster sugar
^{1}/2 teaspoon ground cinnamon
1 teaspoon sea salt
^{1}/2 cup freshly grated coconut
250 ml/9 fl oz coconut milk
sunflower oil, for deep-frying
4 bananas, cut diagonally into
    3 cm/1^1/4 in slices
ice-cream and golden syrup, to serve

1. To make the batter, combine the cornflour, rice flour, sesame seeds, sugar, cinnamon and salt in a mixing bowl, and mix in the grated coconut and coconut milk.

2. Half fill a large wok with sunflower oil and heat to 180°C/350°F. If you don't have a thermometer, a piece of bread will fry to golden brown in about 1 minute when at the correct temperature.

3. Working with a few at a time, dredge the banana slices in the batter, ensuring they are completely covered, then lower into the oil and cook for 1 minute or until golden brown.

4. Lift out with a slotted spoon and drain on paper towels. Best served hot, with ice-cream and golden syrup.

Ben O'Donoghue

Crêpes with caramelised mango and mango ice-cream

As an alternative to the wonderful classic, crêpes suzette, the mangoes in this dish are just fantastic.

SERVES 4

Crêpes
125 g/4¹/₂ oz plain flour, sifted
15 g/¹/₂ oz caster sugar
pinch of salt
2 eggs
325 ml/11¹/₂ fl oz milk
100 g/3¹/₂ oz pouring cream
20 g/³/₄oz butter

150 g/5¹/₂ oz caster sugar
125 g/4¹/₂ oz pouring cream
4 mangoes, peeled and thinly sliced
1 vanilla bean, split in half
100 g/3¹/₂ oz mascarpone cheese
4 scoops mango ice-cream
icing sugar, for dusting

1. To make the crêpes, combine the flour, sugar and salt in a mixing bowl. Add the eggs and whisk until smooth. Combine the milk and cream in a jug and slowly add to the flour mixture to ensure a smooth batter. Strain. Allow to stand for 30 minutes.

2. Heat a crêpe pan or a large non-stick frying pan on medium heat. Brush the pan with a little butter and add enough batter to thinly cover the surface. Once small bubbles appear on top of the crêpe, turn it over. Cook on the opposite side for 30 seconds.

3. Melt the sugar in a heavy-based saucepan over medium heat. Once the sugar has liquefied and started to turn golden brown, add 2 tablespoons of the cream and swirl the pan. Add the mango, the remaining cream and the vanilla bean. Cook for 2–3 minutes.

4. Lay a crêpe on a serving plate. Spread a spoonful of mascarpone over the crêpe and spoon 4–5 slices of caramelised mango onto one quarter. Fold in half and half again to create a small pocket. Placing 3 crêpes on each plate.

5. Place a scoop of mango ice-cream on top of the crêpes. Spoon over the remaining mango slices and drizzle over the sauce. Dust with icing sugar and serve.

Note: The crêpes can be made up to an hour in advance.

Curtis Stone

Mornington Peninsula

Mornington Peninsula
City weekenders and farm workers

The Mornington Peninsula is about an hours' drive east of Melbourne in Australia's southeast. Surrounded on three sides by water, its climate is mild, and regular rains keep it lush and green. It's one of the Melbourne giltterati's favourite places to have a weekender. And it's also home to remarkable produce and wines: 170 vineyards and 54 wineries for starters.

The area reminded us of England: very conservative European-style houses, a soft climate (actually it rained most of the time we were there), plus there are touches of a bygone era like neatly trimmed hedgerows and brightly coloured bathing boxes that are still popular around the bay. This was part of Curtis's stomping ground when he grew up in Melbourne.

Herronswood is a seed-savers headquarters, specialising in heirloom plants. What that means is that they find fruit and vegetables in their original, unadulterated, uncrossed forms, then propagate them and send the seeds worldwide. Thus there are many seeds and plants, previously thought to have been lost to us, now growing in profusion, reinvigorating the gene base of edible plants.

For example, carrots were originally purple; the original cauliflower was yellow; and there were once 3000 varieties of tomatoes, yet mainstream seed merchants concentrate on just six or eight. Remember how tomatoes used to taste before supermarkets insisted on perfect-looking cardboard-tasting lumps? Tomatoes, real tomatoes, that's what Herronswood has. That's what we loved.

At Herronswood, they believe the best way to ensure the integrity of your own food is to grow it yourself. Herronswood is a living catalogue of herbs and vegetables situated on two hectares of formal gardens and home to the Digger's Club.

Then there's Nedlands Farm, a lavender farm. Now while most people think of lavender as something to hang up in the kitchen to create a cosy cottage-kitchen look and aroma, there are

certain types that are said to have medicinal and antibacterial properties and can assist in the treatment of all sorts of ailments.

But as we're chefs and not doctors, what interested us is the fact that they also grow culinary lavender, *Lavandula angustifolia*. Only the flowers are used. Lavender's sweet smell and low camphor content make it ideal as a food ingredient, in much the same way as you'd use a herb or spice.

Next we headed to Montalto vineyard, initially in search of some wine. It is a spectacular 20-hectare property that forms a natural amphitheatre and incorporates 9 hectares of premium vines, 1500 olive trees, extensive wetlands and bird life, and a fruit-and-nut grove plus kitchen gardens for its restaurant.

Owner John Mitchell's pride and joy is his couta (short for 'barracouta') boat. Designed in the 1850s, couta boats are half work-boat, half racer. They had to be because, after a day's fishing, the first boat to make it back to the fishmarkets would get the best price.

Even as recently as 30 years ago, the sight of couta boats on Port Philip Bay had almost disappeared until people like John and his boat-builder mate Tim Phillips became involved. Today this class of boat has been reborn, and up to 80 of them can be seen sailing and racing around Mornington Peninsula.

Tim's a great bloke, someone we felt we'd known all our lives. A real rogue, a seadog, a lovable pirate. Our kind of guy. John, by comparison, is the epitomy of a British sea captain, charming, eloquent. Yet he and Tim share a passion and that's what's made them great mates. And great mates of ours.

While on the peninsula we found what we believe to be some of the best cheeses in Australia. Red Hill farm has a small cheesery and cellar, and Trevor and Jan Brandon produce distinctive handcrafted regional cheeses to complement Mornington Peninsula wines. They were first inspired by farmhouse cheese-making in Europe. Remarkably, they learnt a lot of their craft from books, although Trevor's experience as a food microbiologist undoubtedly helped.

Fully organic, the Red Hill Cheesery produces a range of cheeses including soft cheeses with a white coat, rich, creamy flavours, distinctive tang and pleasantly stimulating aroma. Ready to eat, though mild, at around 3 weeks, they're unforgettable after six weeks of age, when golden flora influences the bouquet and flavour.

Chicken-liver parfait with sour cherry compote

A parfait is a posh way to make a pâté. This recipe takes a bit of time, but the velvety texture and amazing taste make it completely worthwhile.

SERVES 8

4 shallots (eschalots), sliced

1 sprig of thyme

2 garlic cloves, crushed

100 ml/3^1/2 fl oz cognac

100 ml/3^1/2 fl oz port

250 g/9 oz chicken livers, trimmed of
   sinew and fat

4^1/2 eggs (the half egg made up of ^{1}/2 a yolk
   and ^{1}/2 a white), lightly beaten

200 g/7 oz butter, melted

sea salt and freshly ground black pepper

Compote

300 g/11 oz canned sour cherries,
   juice reserved

25 g/1 oz sugar

2 cloves

2 tablespoons cornflour

2 tablespoons water

1 loaf of crusty bread, thinly sliced and
   chargrilled

1. Preheat the oven to 130°C/265°F/Gas Mark ^{1}/2 .

2. Combine the shallots, thyme, garlic, cognac and port in a small saucepan and reduce to a syrup over a medium heat. Allow to cool.

3. Place the chicken livers in a container, pour over the syrup and cover. Allow to marinate in the refrigerator for 2 hours.

4. Transfer the chicken livers and the marinade to a food processor and process for 1–2 minutes, or until reasonably smooth. With the motor running, add the eggs a little at a time. Once the eggs are mixed in, slowly add the melted butter. Strain through a fine sieve. Season with salt and pepper and pour into a 3^1/2-cup capacity terrine mould.

5. Place the terrine mould in a bain-marie (a baking dish filled with cold water to come halfway up the sides of the terrine mould). Cover the terrine mould with foil and place in the oven for 60 minutes. Remove from the oven and transfer to the refrigerator to set for 4–5 hours.

continued over...

Curtis Stone

6   To make the compote, combine the cherries and their juice with the sugar and cloves in a sauce-pan and bring to the boil. Reduce to a simmer.

7   Mix together the cornflour and water to form a paste. Slowly add just enough to the simmering cherries to achieve the consistency of a thin syrup. Remove from the heat and allow to cool.

8   Spoon the chicken liver parfait on to serving plates. Serve with the compote and chargrilled crusty bread.

Curtis Stone

Creamed cauliflower and stilton soup

I cook this soup for all my mates in London on Christmas Day. It is perfect for the cold weather or for festive times. So, Jodie G and Crazy Jane, this one's for you!

SERVES 4

1 large head of cauliflower
1 tablespoon olive oil
2 shallots (eschalots), finely chopped
2 garlic cloves, finely chopped
1 L/1^3/4 pints chicken stock
300 ml/10^1/2 fl oz pouring cream
90 g/3^1/4 oz stilton or similar firm blue
    cheese, diced into 2 cm/^{3}/4 in cubes,
    (set aside 12 cubes for the garnish)
50 g/2 oz plain flour
2^1/2 tablespoons ice-cold water
sunflower oil, for deep-frying

1. Trim the cauliflower into florets, discarding the central stalk.

2. Heat the olive oil in a large saucepan over medium heat, add the shallots and garlic and sweat, without colouring, for 2 minutes. Add the cauliflower florets, reserving 12 for the garnish. Pour in just enough of the chicken stock to cover the cauliflower and cook until tender, 15–20 minutes. Remove from the heat and strain, reserving the stock.

3. Place the cauliflower in a blender and use just enough of the reserved stock to make a smooth puree. Pass through a fine strainer. Return to the heat, add the cream and stilton, and enough of the reserved stock to create the desired consistency of soup.

4. Mix the flour with the water to make a batter for the reserved cauliflower florets and cheese cubes.

5. Heat the sunflower oil in a wok to 180°C/350°F*. Dip the cauliflower florets and the cheese cubes in the batter, shake off the excess batter and deep-fry the florets and cheese until golden. Drain on paper towel.

6. Pour the soup into four warmed serving bowls, garnish with the deep-fried cauliflower and cheese cubes and serve.

*If you don't have a thermometer, drop in a small piece of bread, which will fry to golden brown in 1 minute at the correct temperature.

Curtis Stone

Steamed scallops in the shell with spiced carrot puree and vermicelli noodles

This is a recipe that I have reworked from when I was the chef at Monte's. There is a hint of North Africa at work here, and it suits the sweet scallops well.

SERVES 4

Carrot puree

4 medium carrots, peeled and sliced
100 g/3¹/₂ oz butter, chopped
sea salt
juice of 1 orange
¹/₄ teaspoon ground cumin
sea salt and freshly ground black pepper

50 g/2 oz rice vermicelli noodles

Scallops

12 large scallops in the shell
¹/₂ teaspoon ground cinnamon
finely grated zest of 1 orange
¹/₂ teaspoon dried chilli flakes

olive oil, to drizzle
1 witlof (endive), finely sliced
handful of coriander leaves, to garnish

1. To make the carrot puree, place the carrots in a saucepan and just cover with water. Add the butter, season with salt and cook, partially covered, over a low heat for 10 minutes or until very tender and sweet. Drain, transfer to a food processor and puree. While still hot, add the orange juice and cumin and season with salt and pepper. Keep warm.

2. Soak the noodles in boiling water for 5 minutes, drain and refresh.

3. Remove the scallops from the shells, and clean by rinsing under cold running water. Clean and dry the scallop shells and arrange on a serving platter. Season each scallop with a pinch of the combined cinnamon, orange zest and chilli flakes. Place the scallops in a steamer and steam for 2–3 minutes or until they just change colour.

4. Warm the noodles in the carrot puree and divide between the scallop shells. Drizzle over a little olive oil — the noodles should be loose and full of juice. Place a scallop on top of the noodles, garnish with a little witlof and coriander and serve.

Ben O'Donoghue

Ceviche of salmon with fennel cream

The combination of a fat fish, such as salmon, and lime juice works so well. The added richness of creamed fennel and the salty pearls of salmon caviar make this dish into a real treat. This recipe is always well received at my restaurant.

SERVES 4

Fennel cream

1 large fennel bulb, finely sliced
1 teaspoon fennel seeds
250 ml/9 fl oz dry white wine
500 ml/18 fl oz pouring cream
squeeze of lemon juice
sea salt and freshly ground white pepper

Ceviche

500 g/1 lb 2 oz salmon fillet
juice of 2 limes
sea salt

Garnish

olive oil, to drizzle
4 heaped teaspoons salmon caviar
cress or mustard cress, leaves picked

1. To make the fennel cream, place the fennel, fennel seeds and white wine in a saucepan and cook, covered, for 10 minutes or until soft. Add the cream and cook, uncovered, for 5 minutes or until reduced and very thick. Using a hand blender, puree until smooth. Season with the lemon juice, salt and pepper and allow to cool.

2. To make the ceviche, cut across the salmon fillet into slices about 1 cm/^{1}/$_3$ in thick. Place in a shallow ceramic dish and pour over the lime juice, making sure the fish is evenly covered. Season with salt, using a little more than you usually would as it works well with the lime juice. Cover and leave in the fridge to marinate for 20 minutes or until opaque.

3. Arrange the salmon in a circle on serving plates and pipe on the fennel cream (using a squeeze bottle or a paper piping bag). Drizzle over a little olive oil. Place a generous teaspoon of the salmon caviar in the middle and scatter the cress leaves around the plate.

Ben O'Donoghue

Roast beetroot and goats' curd salad

Beetroot is just about my favourite vegetable. Served with a fresh, tart goats cheese and fresh herbs you are well on your way to heaven in a salad.

SERVES 4

12 small beetroot
2–3 tablespoons good olive oil
sea salt and freshly ground black pepper
leaves of $^1/_4$ bunch of thyme
125 ml/4$^1/_2$ fl oz balsamic vinegar
leaves of $^1/_4$ bunch of dill
leaves of $^1/_4$ bunch of tarragon
1 frisée, white part only
60 g/2$^1/_4$ oz fresh goats' curd or soft goats' cheese, seasoned with salt and pepper and a squeeze of lemon juice
1 lemon, to squeeze

1 Preheat the oven to 180°C/350°F/Gas Mark 4.

2 Scrub the beetroot and leave on the tops and tails so that they don't bleed and lose flavour while cooking. Toss in a baking dish with the olive oil, salt, pepper, thyme and three-quarters of the balsamic vinegar. Cover with foil, place in the oven and cook for 1 hour or until tender. Uncover and roast until the beetroot starts to crisp in parts. Leave to cool. Remove any burnt bits and cut the beets into chunks — halves or quarters, depending on the size of the beet — to reveal the colour.

3 Arrange the beetroot on serving plates, scatter over the dill, tarragon and frisée leaves and crumble the goats' curd over the top.

4 Drizzle the whole salad with the remaining balsamic vinegar, the beetroot juices from the roasting tray, a little extra olive oil and a squeeze of lemon juice and serve.

Ben O'Donoghue

Flathead with a citrus and pepper rub, spinach and pomme écrassé

I thought of this recipe because I hate wasting food. It bugged me that I was always throwing out the zest of citrus fruit, so I came up with a use for it. This fish dish is the result!

SERVES 4

4 oranges
4 lemons
2 limes
10 roasted coriander seeds
10 black peppercorns
pinch of sea salt
pinch of sugar
extra virgin olive oil
4 (approximately 200 g/7 oz total) potatoes,
  left whole
75 ml/2^1/$_2$ fl oz olive oil
1 tablespoon finely sliced flat leaf parsley
12 x 100 g/3^1/$_2$ oz flathead fillets
100 g/3^1/$_2$ oz spinach
25 g/1 oz butter

1. Zest oranges, lemons and limes. Remove any bitter pith from zest. Set fruit aside.

2. Spread zest on a metal tray and place in direct sunlight and allow to dry for 12–24 hours. When dried, put in a food processor with coriander seeds, peppercorns, sugar and salt and process until the mixture resembles breadcrumbs. Set aside.

3. Preheat the oven to 180°C/350°F/Gas Mark 4.

4. To make the sauce vierge, juice the set aside citrus fruits. Measure the juice then slowly add an equal quantity of extra virgin olive oil, whisking continually.

5. To make the pomme écrassé, boil potatoes until tender. Remove skin and crush potato with a fork. Add the olive oil and parsley. Keep warm.

6. In a hot pan, cook flathead fillets in a little olive oil on one side until golden brown. Turn carefully with a spatula. Sprinkle over the citrus rub and drizzle with olive oil. Finish in the oven for 30 seconds to 1 minute.

continued opposite...

7 Wilt spinach with butter in a separate pre-heated pan. Once the spinach is wilted, squeeze out excess moisture and spread on serving plate. Spoon potato at the back of the plate and arrange flathead fillets over the top. Spoon sauce vierge around the edge of the plate to finish.

Roasted guinea fowl with goats' cheese, lemon and rosemary

The theme of this recipe revolves around the wine, the grape and the cheese: the wine is sauvignon blanc, the grape is white, and the cheese is goats'.

SERVES 4

2 x 900 g/2 lb guinea fowls
2 teaspoons chopped rosemary
250 g/9 oz soft goats' cheese
juice of 1 lemon
2 tablespoons olive oil
6 extra sprigs of rosemary
1 lemon, quartered

Garnish

250 g/9 oz shallots (eschalots), thinly sliced
1 bulb of garlic, cloves separated, root ends
    removed and skins left on
6 sprigs of rosemary
300 g/11 oz seedless white grapes
250 ml/9 fl oz sauvignon blanc
sea salt and freshly ground black pepper
50 g/2 oz butter, diced

steamed spinach and toasted pine nuts,
    to serve

1. Preheat the oven to 220°C/425°F/Gas Mark 7.

2. Trim any excess fat from the guinea fowls and remove the wishbones. Beginning from the neck end of each bird, use your index and middle finger to push your hand between the skin and meat of both breasts and thighs to separate the skin from the flesh and to create a pocket.

3. Combine the chopped rosemary with the goats' cheese, lemon juice and olive oil. Push the goats' cheese mixture into the pocket. Press the outside of each bird to spread the mixture evenly under the skin. Place 3 sprigs of rosemary and 2 lemon quarters into the cavity of each bird.

4. Scatter the shallots, garlic cloves and rosemary in a baking tray and place the birds breast-up on top. Place in the oven and roast for 15 minutes to colour. Reduce the heat to 140°C/275°F/Gas Mark 1 and cook for 20 minutes. Turn the birds over, add the grapes and wine and cook for another 25 minutes.

Ben O'Donoghue

⑤ Remove from the oven and allow to rest for 10 minutes. Remove the breast and thigh from each carcass, carve into quarters and place on warmed serving plates. Remove the skin from the garlic cloves.

⑥ Pour the pan juices, grapes and peeled garlic cloves (not the rosemary) into a saucepan. Bring to the boil. Gradually whisk in the butter until the sauce has thickened, season and pour over the meat. Serve with steamed spinach and pine nuts.

Oven-roasted fillet of beef with wild mushrooms and pan-fried foie gras

The real name for this dish is Beef Rossini, brought to use by the famous composer who wrote William Tell. Between you and me, I think he was better with his food than his music.

SERVES 4

2 tablespoons olive oil

4 x 200 g/7 oz beef eye fillet steaks

2 shallots (eschalots), finely sliced

2 garlic cloves, finely chopped

200 g/7 oz assorted wild mushrooms,
    (morels, Swiss browns, pine)

1 tablespoon finely chopped flat leaf parsley

50 g/2 oz butter

4 x 1 cm/$^1/_3$ in thick slices sourdough bread

200 g/7 oz picked spinach leaves

4 escalopes of foie gras from a lobe, each
    weighing 30–50 g/1–2 oz

1 quantity red wine sauce, warmed
    (see Poached lamb loin on page 28)

1. Preheat the oven to 200°C/400°F/Gas Mark 6.

2. Heat 1 tablespoon of the olive oil in a heavy-based frying pan on high heat. Add the steaks and cook for 1 minute on each side to seal. Transfer to an oven tray and place in the oven for 8 minutes for medium-rare (depending on thickness).

3. Meanwhile, heat the remaining oil in the same pan, add the shallots and cook for 1 minute. Add the garlic, mushrooms and parsley and cook for a further 2–3 minutes. Set aside and keep warm.

4. In a separate frying pan, melt half the butter, add the sourdough slices and pan-fry for 1 minute on each side. Set aside and keep warm.

5. In the same pan, melt the remaining butter, add the spinach leaves and toss until just wilted.

6. Sauté the foie gras lobes in a hot dry pan for 20 seconds on each side.

7. Place an 11.5 cm/4$^1/_2$ in cutter on a plate and put one quarter of the spinach inside. Carefully remove. Cut a slice of the fried sourdough with a 10 cm/4 in cutter and put on top of the spinach. Follow with a steak. Top with foie gras, then spoon the mushroom mixture around the outside of each plate, season with salt and pepper and drizzle with the warmed red wine sauce.

Curtis Stone

Lavender crème brûlée

Crème brûlées are a timeless classic. This is a very romantic variation, so if you are wanting to impress, give it a go!

SERVES 4

3 egg yolks
1 egg
100 ml/3½ fl oz milk
450 ml/¾ pint pouring cream
75 g/2¾ oz caster sugar
5 stems English lavender*, stalks removed
1 vanilla bean, halved lengthways and
*   seeds scraped*
2 tablespoons demerara sugar

1. Place the egg yolks, egg and 1 tablespoon of the milk in a bowl and whisk lightly to combine.

2. Place the remaining milk, the cream, sugar, lavender, vanilla seeds and bean in a saucepan over a low heat and stir until the sugar is dissolved. Remove the lavender and discard. Increase the heat to medium and stir until the mixture almost comes to the boil. Remove from the heat and gradually pour over the egg mixture, whisking to combine. Return to the saucepan and whisk over a low heat for 5–6 minutes or until thickened (almost as thick as a custard). Be careful not to scramble the mixture.

3. Strain the lavender custard into a jug and pour into a large 1-L/1¾-pint serving dish or four individual 1-cup capacity ramekins. Refrigerate until chilled.

4. Sprinkle the demerara sugar over the top and transfer to a baking dish filled with ice. Place under a hot grill for 1–2 minutes to caramelise the sugar and serve.

* English lavender can be picked from the garden as long as it is pesticide free.

Baked apricot cheesecake

I think that you are better off making your own jam with this one since then you will have loads of apricot jam left over — never a bad thing. You can, of course, use a good quality bought variety. Just make sure the jam is runny so you can pour it!

SERVES 4

Sponge base

125 g/4¹/₂ oz butter

¹/₂ cup caster sugar

1 vanilla pod, split lengthways and
    seeds scraped

2 eggs

1 teaspoon finely grated lemon zest

1 tablespoon milk

1 cup plain flour, sifted

1 teaspoon baking powder, sifted

¹/₂ teaspoon salt

Filling

250 g/9 oz soft goats' cheese

250 g/9 oz sour cream

1 cup caster sugar

4 eggs

¹/₂ cup good apricot jam, thinned a
    little with water and warmed to the
    consistency of a coulis

1. Preheat the oven to 180°C/350°F/Gas Mark 4. Grease and line a 23-cm/9-in springform tin with greaseproof baking paper.

2. To make the sponge base, cream the butter, sugar and vanilla seeds until light and creamy. Beat in the eggs, one at a time, until well incorporated. Add the lemon zest and milk and mix well. Fold in the dry ingredients and pour into the prepared tin.

3. To make the filling, beat the goats' cheese and sour cream in a mixing bowl until smooth, about 5 minutes. Beat in the sugar and eggs until well incorporated.

4. Pour some of the warm jam over the sponge base and then pour over the filling. Add another layer of warm jam on top. The different layers of sponge, jam and filling will marble as the cheesecake cooks.

5. Place in the oven and bake for 35–40 minutes or until lightly golden and still a bit wobbly. Allow to cool and serve with a little more thinned, warm jam.

Ben O'Donoghue

Ningaloo Reef

Ningaloo Reef

Where the outback meets the sea

Ningaloo Reef is a pristine environment that runs 260 kilometres along the coast of Western Australia from Exmouth in the north, past Coral Bay in the south. Indigenous Australians have been here for tens of thousands of years. The Dutch first visited the region in 1618, but it was many more years before anyone thought to settle there. The reefs that protect the coast are also the graves of many a sailing ship that miscalculated its position on its way to the Dutch East Indies and the Spice Islands. The reef is currently under consideration for World Heritage listing, and from what we saw, we say 'Dead right'.

Coral Bay was a good starting point because the reef actually comes right into the shore there. You can snorkel and see exotic fish and stunning coral in waist-deep water. Kids even feed huge snappers by hand in knee-deep water by the shore.

Out on the reef we saw bream, shark, snapper (pink, black, nor-west), dhufish, coral trout, blue bone or baldchin groper (one of the best eating fish on the planet), cod, whiting and mackerel. Unbelievable. On the reef itself, they're protected. You have to go beyond the reef if you want to fish. Out there you can also find tuna, marlin and sailfish. How's that for an incentive? Up that way you'll also find crabs (blue manna, swimmers, snow crabs, mud crabs), prawns and scallops. It'd be hard to go hungry up there.

There were also dolphin pods, but the most exciting thing was swimming with giant manta rays close by. These creatures are awesome — some are up to 7 metres across. They move through the water like birds in flight with a gentle swoosh of their wings. And we were right there with them. That was unforgettable.

Two hours from Coral Bay is Carnarvon, across the Tropic of Capricorn. The countryside is quite surreal up there. The land is so flat that the horizon appears as a perfectly straight line way off in the distance. And the sky is big, bright and blue. Barely a cloud to be seen. Even though the region grows loads of produce, it's officially a desert.

Along this coastline, however, are some of the world's best waves. In fact, a leg of the world surfing tournament is held up this way. Just our luck, the day we were there it was a full moon and a really low tide. We still went in for a surf, but most locals didn't even bother, that's how spoilt they are. Although seeing four whales frolicking within 100 metres of us made up for that disappointment.

We also called in at Quobba Station, home of the Meecham family. The homestead sits right on the ocean's edge with the red dirt going right down to the white sand-and-shell beach. This truly is where the outback meets the sea. The Dorpa sheep on this station are reared just for meat as the bottom has fallen out of the wool industry. In fact, these sheep don't even have wool, just a kind of shag like a goat.

Not far from Quobba is the Lake McLeod salt mine. And as salt is a chef's constant cooking companion, we went in for a quick look. The process really is quite amazing.

Lake McLeod is a salt lake about 2072 square kilometres in area. But deep below, laid down millions of years ago by an ancient sea is a brine of salt and water, nine times saltier than the ocean. This is pumped into massive holding pools on the surface of the lake where the relentless sun evaporates the water and leaves the salt behind. Pure salt. One of the purest natural sources of salt in the world we were told. More than 99 per cent pure when dry. From this facility alone they export over one million tonnes of salt every year.

Due east of Carnarvon and nestled in the foothills of the spectacular and rugged Kennedy Ranges, the Maslins own Mardathuna Station. It's desert country out there. Red-earthed, scrubby and dry, it's pretty tough for animals to get a feed and their only water comes from windmill-driven pumps spread out across the land. But after the annual rains, the entire place is transformed almost overnight into a lush green land of grasses and colourful wildflowers.

Out there the cattle eat native grasses and an introduced species, Buffel grass. Buffel grass first made its way to Australia in the very early days of exploration; it was the natural padding in the Afghan camel driver's saddles. The Afghans, with their camels, were instrumental in helping explorers and settlers open up these lands to agriculture. Today it's not unusual to see their legacy — wild camels — in the outback and in the desert.

Another introduced species that has thrived in this inhospitable environment is the goat. Once pests to be controlled, now they're more valuable than sheep. These rangeland goats, most of which have never seen a person before, survive and thrive out there. Their meat is a little gamey, but delicious and natural. Goat is the largest individually eaten meat in the world. In Australia, the demand is growing and there's always a big export market, too.

The cattle out at the station are basically organic. No chemicals are used to enhance the soil, just nature's whims.

Carnarvon itself was first settled in 1876 and was established as a port town for the export of wool and livestock. Due to the big tides, the jetty is about 1.6 kilometres in length so ships can remain in deep water. Carnarvon is also the food-bowl of the west and Perth's main winter supply of fruit and vegetables.

The Gascoyne River that flows through Carnarvon is also known as 'the upside down river'. It flows only occasionally between February and August, but there's always loads of water under the riverbed. More than enough water to pump out for the 162 or so plantations that grow everything from bananas, mangoes, avocadoes, papaya/pawpaw, watermelon, table grapes and all manner of vegetables including lettuce, tomatoes, capsicum, chillies and beans.

There's another reason it's so fertile. The catchment of this river is some 500 kilometres inland in the mineral-rich desert interior. When it rains, it pours, and the river brings down minerals and goodness that, when the river breaks its banks, floods the classic river delta, enriching it as it does.

Many of the market gardeners are immigrant Australians, mainly from Yugoslavia (as it was), Italy, Portugal and, latterly, Vietnam. They all work hard under the hot sun and reap the rewards.

We visited Tiago DaDrue, a Portuguese–Australian who made excellent 'sugar-bah' (shishkebab): small chunks of meat marinated in Portuguese wine and garlic and slowly turned on sword-like skewers over hot coals.

As well, we met Croatian-born Tom Yelash. He plucked some magnificent specimens of eggplant (aubergine) from his field, sliced them thinly, dusted them with paprika and turned them regularly on the hot plate. A filling of feta, garlic and a dash of white wine was added and the result was classic Mediterranean flavour. So robust and tasty.

More than 3500 tonnes of prawns are brought ashore every year in Carnarvon. That's 60 per cent of the state's prawn and scallops catch. And the prawns here are huge — kings and tigers — they look more like small lobsters!

A great prawning innovation from this region has been the development of turtle, dolphin and shark-friendly nets. These nets have been designed with a simple escape hatch so that large creatures, well, larger than a prawn anyway, are simply spat out as the nets move along.

Rodeos are still big events in the outback. People come from hundreds of kilometres away. We couldn't help but get involved with the annual Carnarvon Rodeo, so Ben took on the role of Rodeo Clown (now that's typecasting, isn't it?), which resulted in a few hairy moments when the bull thought Ben's colourful garb deserved a closer look. And Curtis had a go at the barrel race. That's where you guide the horse around a number of barrels in a particular order. We won't tell you his time, because that would be embarrassing, but at least he didn't fall off! And we count that as a win.

Watermelon gazpacho

This is a funky twist on a classic recipe that does really well as a light summer starter. The flavour combinations work really well together.

SERVES 6

1 watermelon, weighing about
   3 kg/6 lb 9 $^3/_4$ oz, peeled and deseeded
1 large cucumber, peeled and deseeded
1 red onion
2 tablespoons ground almonds
250 g/9 oz white seedless grapes, chopped
3 teaspoons chopped mint
$^1/_2$ French stick, cut into 6 slices
1 garlic clove, peeled and halved
extra virgin olive oil
sea salt and freshly ground black pepper
3 tablespoons soft goats' cheese
1–2 tablespoons red wine vinegar
extra virgin olive oil, to drizzle
extra chopped mint, to garnish

1. Place the watermelon, half the cucumber, half the red onion and the ground almonds in a food processor and puree. Pour into a bowl and place in the fridge to chill completely.

2. Finely chop the remaining cucumber and onion and mix with the grapes and mint. Place in the fridge to chill.

3. Toast the bread slices, rub with the garlic and drizzle over the olive oil. Season with the salt and pepper and spread with the goats' cheese.

4. Just before serving, season the watermelon gazpacho with the red wine vinegar until it just balances with the sweetness of the fruit.

5. Divide the grape mixture and then the soup equally between six soup bowls. Float a crouton on top of each and drizzle over a little extra virgin olive oil. Garnish with some extra chopped mint.

Ben O'Donoghue

Barbecued king prawns with dill and lemon butter

One of the things most frequently said to me as an Aussie chef living and working abroad is, 'Throw another prawn on the barbie.' And, to be honest, I had never really tried. But you know what? It's fantastic.

SERVES 4

Dill and lemon butter

250 g/9 oz unsalted butter, softened
1 tablespoon finely chopped fresh dill
2 garlic cloves, crushed
1 small shallot (eschalot), finely chopped
1 tablespoon finely chopped flat leaf parsley
sea salt and freshly ground black pepper
juice of $^1/_2$ lemon
1 tablespoon Pernod

12 extra large green king prawns
1 lemon, quartered, to garnish

1. To make the dill and lemon butter, combine the butter, dill, garlic, shallot, parsley, salt, pepper, lemon juice and Pernod in a bowl and mix well.

2. Butterfly the prawns by slicing along the belly, leaving the shell intact.

3. Evenly spread a heaped tablespoon of the dill and lemon butter onto the exposed prawn flesh.

4. Preheat the barbecue or, alternatively, a grill to high.

5. Place each prawn, flesh-side down, onto a hot chargrill for 1–2 minutes. Or transfer the prawns to a large baking tray and place under the grill for 2–3 minutes or until cooked through.

6. Divide the prawns between four warmed plates and serve, garnished with the lemon quarters.

Curtis Stone

King prawn laksa

This recipe is a wonderful combination of spices and the richness of coconut. It can be a great success either as a main course for 4 or a small starter for 8 people. If you don't have time to make the spice mix, just use a good curry powder.

SERVES 4

500 ml/18 fl oz coconut milk

50 g/2 oz ginger

2 garlic cloves

4–5 shallots (echalots)

$^1\!/_2$ bunch coriander, washed, roots and
    leaves and separated

1 teaspoon ground turmeric

1–2 teaspoons garam masala

$1^1\!/_2$ teaspoons ground coriander

1 teaspoon ground bay or 1 bay leaf

$^1\!/_2$ teaspoon ground cardamom

1 teaspoon ground cumin

$^1\!/_4$ teaspoon ground black pepper

$^1\!/_4$ teaspoon ground cinnamon

$^1\!/_4$ teaspoon ground cloves

3–4 kaffir lime leaves

12 green king prawns, peeled except for
    the tail

2 tablespoons light soy sauce

1 L/1$^3\!/_4$ pints chicken stock

sea salt and freshly ground black pepper

600 g/1 lb 5$^1\!/_4$ oz egg noodles

Garnish salad

1 witlof (endive), finely sliced

1 small fennel bulb, finely sliced

1 nashi pear, finely sliced

4 fried long red dried chillies

crisp fried onion

1 lime, quartered

1. Place the coconut milk in a wok over a medium heat. Bring to the boil and cook for about 10 minutes until it splits (turns into an oil).

2. Puree the ginger, garlic, shallots and coriander roots using a mortar and pestle. Add to the coconut oil and fry for 1 minute. Add the spices and lime leaves and fry until fragrant, then add the prawns and soy sauce. Add the chicken stock and bring to a simmer. Adjust the seasoning by adding the salt and pepper.

3. Cook the noodles in a large pot of boiling water until just tender, and divide between four serving bowls. Ladle the broth over, and top with the prawns.

4. Combine the witlof, fennel and pear. Fill 4 small bowls with the salad and sprinkle a little over the laksa. Sprinkle some fried chillies and crisp fried onion over the soup as well. Serve the soup with the little bowls of salad and a wedge of lime.

Ben O'Donoghue

Garganelli with mixed fish stew

This is the type of stew you would expect to be served somewhere along the coast of southern Italy. It is simple, rustic and tasty.

SERVES 4

Fish stew

100 ml/3¹/₂ fl oz olive oil

4 shallots (eschalots), finely chopped

2 garlic cloves, crushed

100 ml/3¹/₂ fl oz white wine

2 x 400 g/14 oz canned tomatoes,
    seeds removed

2 tablespoons baby capers (if salted, soak
    in cold water for 30 minutes and rinse
    well)

100 g/3¹/₂ oz kalamata olives

2 bay leaves

1 sprig of thyme

4 extra large green king prawns, peeled,
    de-veined and halved lengthwise

300 g/11 oz small red mullet, reef fish,
    groper, cod, whiting fillets, halved

¹/₂ cup basil leaves, torn

salt and freshly ground black pepper

400 g/14 oz garganelli

extra virgin olive oil, to drizzle

sea salt

small basil leaves, to garnish

1. To make the fish stew, heat 1 tablespoon of the olive oil in a large saucepan over medium heat. Add the shallots and garlic and cook for 1–2 minutes to soften. Add the white wine and stir to deglaze the pan. Add the tomatoes, capers, olives, bay leaves and thyme, reduce heat to low and simmer for 20 minutes. Add the prawns and cook for 2 minutes. Add the fish fillets and cook for 2–3 minutes or until just cooked through. Stir through the torn basil and the remaining olive oil and season with salt and pepper.

2. Bring a large saucepan of salted water to the boil. Add the garganelli and cook for 10–12 minutes or until *al dente*. Drain and place in a large warmed serving bowl. Drizzle over a little extra virgin olive oil. Season with the sea salt and arrange the fish stew on top of the garganelli. Garnish with small basil leaves and serve with crusty bread.

Curtis Stone

Fresh tagliatelle with ragu of kid

Both domestic and wild goat is eaten widely in Italy — and the Caribbean, for that matter. It has a lovely taste, similar to lamb, although perhaps a little lighter, so don't be afraid to try it.

SERVES 4

2 tablespoons olive oil

1.4 kg/3 lb 1¼ oz leg of kid (goat) or lamb

4 shallots (eschalots), roughly chopped

4 garlic cloves, crushed

1 carrot, roughly chopped

1 celery stick, roughly chopped

250 ml/9 fl oz red wine

1 L/1¾ pints veal stock

juice of 2 oranges

finely grated zest of 1 orange

2 sprigs of thyme

1 sprig of rosemary

3 bay leaves

10 sage leaves, chopped

12 small truss tomatoes, oven roasted

400 g/14 oz fresh tagliatelle

2½ tablespoons extra virgin olive oil

2 tablespoons finely chopped flat leaf parsley

120 g/4¼ oz aged pecorino, shaved

1. Preheat the oven to 150°C/300°F/Gas Mark 2.

2. Heat the oil in a large flameproof casserole dish and brown the kid leg on all sides over medium heat. Remove the kid leg and add the shallots, garlic, carrot and celery and sweat until light brown. Return the kid leg to the casserole dish and deglaze with the red wine. Add the veal stock, orange juice and zest, thyme, rosemary and bay leaves. Cover and place in the oven for 2½–3 hours or until the meat is falling off the bone. Remove from the oven and allow to cool.

3. Using your hands, pick all the meat from the bone, discarding any fat and sinew. Strain the vegetables and bones from the stock. Combine the stock with the meat and add the sage.

4. Increase the heat of the oven to 200°C/400°F/Gas Mark 6 and roast the tomatoes (stems still attached), on a baking tray for 5–10 minutes until soft and the skins split. Remove and set aside.

5. Bring a large pot of salted water to the boil, add the tagliatelle and cook until *al dente*. Transfer the pasta to a large warmed bowl and toss through the extra virgin olive oil, parsley and meat. Serve in warm pasta bowls and garnish with the pecorino and tomatoes.

Curtis Stone

Whole wok-fried snapper

I love Asian cooking, especially the way fish is done. This recipe combines great flavours, simplicity and an absolutely stunning presentation as a shared centrepiece on a table. Make sure that you use only the freshest fish.

SERVES 4

Sauce
125 ml/4½ fl oz rice vinegar
50 g/2 oz caster sugar
2½ tablespoons fish sauce
1 small red chilli, chopped
1 garlic clove, chopped
juice of 1 fresh lime

2 kg/4½ lb whole snapper, scaled, gutted
    and gills removed
2 tablespoons cornflour
½ teaspoon ground turmeric
sea salt
sunflower oil, for frying
3–4 long dried chillies
2 fingers of fresh turmeric, peeled and
    julienned
1 large finger of fresh young ginger,
    peeled and julienned
2 garlic cloves, finely sliced
1 bunch of spring onions, finely sliced
freshly ground black pepper
1–2 finely sliced green chillies
¼ bunch of coriander, leaves picked

1. To make the sauce, bring the rice vinegar and sugar to the boil in a small saucepan, allow to cool and add the rest of the ingredients.

2. Score diagonal cuts across the thickest part of the fish, down to the bone. Pat dry with paper towel.

3. Mix the cornflour, turmeric and salt together and dredge the fish in this mixture.

4. Pour enough sunflower oil into a large wok so that the fish will be just covered. Heat to 150°C/300°F and slowly fry the fish for about 25 minutes or until crisp and cooked through. Lift out the fish, drain well, place on a warmed serving platter and keep warm.

5. Discard all but 2 tablespoons of the oil in the wok, return to the heat. Fry the dried chillies over a high heat for 1 minute, add the turmeric, ginger, garlic and the whites of the spring onions and fry until they start to colour. Season with the black pepper and sprinkle the mixture over the fish. Garnish with the green chillies, spring onion greens and coriander. Serve with the sauce in a small dipping bowl on the side.

Ben O'Donoghue

Steamed snapper with potage of shellfish

I was taught to cook this dish by Spencer Patrick, head chef of the Grill Room and Café Royal in London. No matter how food trends change, this recipe is priceless and never dates.

SERVES 4

Sauce

1 tablespoon olive oil

4 shallots (eschalots), finely chopped

1 sprig of thyme

2 bay leaves

250 ml/9 fl oz white wine

250 ml/9 fl oz Noilly Prat dry vermouth

250 ml/9 fl oz fish stock

300 ml/10½ fl oz cream

4 x 100 g/½ oz small snapper fillets, skin on

100 g/3½ oz mussels, bearded and scrubbed

150 g/5½ oz fresh clams (vongole)

1 blue swimmer crab, cleaned and cut
   into 8 pieces

2 tablespoons water

20 tarragon leaves

4 oysters, removed from shell

25 g/1 oz butter

200 g/7 oz spinach leaves, washed and
   drained

1. To make the sauce, heat the olive oil in a saucepan over medium heat. Add the shallots, thyme and bay leaves and sweat, without colouring, for 1 minute. Add the white wine and reduce to a thick syrup. Add the Noilly Prat and reduce to a thick syrup. Add the fish stock and reduce to a thick syrup once more. Add the cream, reduce heat to low and bring to a simmer. Remove immediately from the heat and strain.

2. Place a piece of baking paper over a round wire rack that fits into a large saucepan. Place the snapper fillets on the paper-lined rack in a single layer, ready to use. Heat the saucepan over high heat. Add the mussels, vongole and crab. Place the rack of snapper fillets over the shellfish. Pour the water down the inside of the saucepan, being careful not to wet the fish. Cover the saucepan immediately and steam for 2 minutes.

3. Pour the sauce down the inside of the saucepan. Add the tarragon leaves and swirl the saucepan to coat the shellfish. Cover and cook for a further 1–2 minutes or until the fish is cooked. Remove the fish from the pan and set aside. Add the oysters to the pan and stir through. Strain the sauce from the pan into a large bowl and, using a hand blender, whisk until frothy.

continued opposite...

Curtis Stone

④ Melt the butter in a large frying pan, add the spinach and toss for 1–2 minutes or until just wilted. Set aside and keep warm.

⑤ Divide the spinach between four serving plates. Arrange the fish and the shellfish, reserving the oysters, over the spinach.

⑥ Place the reserved oysters on top of the fish, spoon the sauce over and around the shellfish and serve.

Curtis Stone

Tagine of goat with dates and almonds

While travelling in Morocco I was totally inspired by the simplicity of the cooking and the superb combination of flavours. This is a great one-pan recipe and an excellent use of tougher cuts of meat. It work really well with lamb, too.

SERVES 4

1 bunch of coriander, washed, roots and
    leaves separated
1 garlic clove, halved
pinch of saffron
$^1/_2$ teaspoon ground turmeric
1 teaspoons ground cumin
1 teaspoons ground ginger
$^1/_2$ teaspoon white pepper
sea salt
750 ml/1 pint 7 fl oz water
juice of 1 lemon
600 g/1 lb 5$^1/_4$ oz shoulder of goat or lamb,
    cut into 3 cm/1$^1/_4$ in cubes
1 medium carrot, cut into 1.5 cm/$^3/_4$ in
    cubes
1 medium red onion, halved and sliced
    lengthways
125 g/4$^1/_2$ oz pitted medjool dates
3 tablespoons argan oil* or peanut
    (groundnut) oil, plus extra to drizzle
1 cinnamon stick
$^1/_2$ cup slivered almonds, toasted

1. Pound the coriander roots, garlic, saffron, turmeric, cumin, ginger and white pepper in a mortar with a little salt. Combine with the water and lemon juice. Place the meat, carrot, onion and dates in a large bowl and pour over the spice mixture. Leave to marinate for 30 minutes.

2. Place a tagine or heavy-based flameproof casserole dish over a low heat and add the argan oil, marinated meat mixture and the cinnamon stick. Cover and simmer gently for 1$^1/_2$–2 hours or until tender. You may need to add a little more liquid; check occasionally during cooking.

3. Toast the almonds in a dry frying pan until golden. Chop the reserved coriander leaves. Garnish the tagine with the almonds, coriander and a little drizzle of argan oil and serve.

* Argan oil is derived from argan nuts that are grown in Morocco and is available from specialist produce shops.

Sea breeze sorbet

An excellent way to consume your favourite cocktail!

SERVES 6

500 ml/18 fl oz cranberry juice
250 ml/9 fl oz pink grapefruit juice
250 g/9 oz caster sugar
100 g/3$\frac{1}{2}$ oz liquid glucose
250 ml/9 fl oz vodka
1 egg white, lightly beaten

1. Heat the cranberry juice, grapefruit juice, sugar, glucose and vodka in a saucepan over a medium heat and stir, without boiling, until the sugar has dissolved. Bring to the boil, then remove from the heat and cool completely in the refrigerator.

2. Transfer the mixture to an ice-cream maker and churn following manufacturer's instructions. Alternatively, pour the mixture into a container, cover, and place in the freezer. When the liquid starts to become icy, whisk it occasionally to break up the ice particles and create a smooth mixture. Repeat the process of freezing and whisking for up to 3 hours for best results.

3. When the mixture is starting to become consistently slushy and frozen, whisk in the egg white. This has a stabilizing effect on the sorbet, binding all the ingredients.

4. Return to the freezer, and freeze until the mixture is thick and 'spoonable', but not solid.

Ben O'Donoghue

Tian of citrus and cream with sweet pastry

This dessert has a variety of flavours and textures. It is sweet, sharp, rich, light, crispy and velvety, all at once.

SERVES 8

Syrup
200 g/7 oz caster sugar
100 ml/3$\frac{1}{2}$ fl oz white rum
2$\frac{1}{2}$ tablespoons mixed citrus juice,
*   caught in a bowl as you are*
*   segmenting the fruit*
6 oranges, segmented
5 ruby grapefruits, segmented
4 lemons, segmented

plain flour to dust
$\frac{1}{2}$ quantity of sweet shortcrust pastry
*   (see Chocolate tart on page 59)*
200 ml/7 fl oz pouring cream
25 g/1 oz marmalade

1. Preheat the oven to 200°C/400°F/Gas Mark 6.

2. To make the syrup, place the sugar in a saucepan over medium heat. Cook until it dissolves and begins to turn golden brown. Remove from the heat and add the rum and citrus juice. Return to the heat and reduce for 2 minutes. Set aside to cool. Add the citrus segments and allow to macerate for 12–24 hours.

3. On a lightly floured work bench, roll out the pastry to 3 cm/1$\frac{1}{4}$ in thick. Cut out 8 discs using a 6 cm/2$\frac{1}{2}$ in round cutter. Place the pastry discs onto a greaseproof paper-lined baking tray and transfer to the oven for 8–10 minutes or until golden.

4. Whisk the cream to stiff peaks with an electric beater.

5. Spread the marmalade over each pastry disc. Position a pastry disc in the centre of each serving plate and place a 6 cm/2$\frac{1}{2}$ in round cutter over each disc. Layer the citrus segments and the cream over each disc, using the cutter as a guide. Drizzle the syrup around each tian and serve.

Curtis Stone

Sydney

Sydney

New beginning in Australia's oldest city

Both Bender and Curtis have worked or lived in Sydney in the past. We were all there for Ben's wedding to Dee. So that meant a lot of planning, and a lot of produce needed to be looked at in detail — after all a wedding feast is mighty important for a chef. Sydney's best-kept produce secret is just an hours' drive away, in the Blue Mountains. Forty per cent of Sydney's fresh fruit and vegetables come from this region.

At the top of the Blue Mountains, west of Sydney, is Mount Tomah Farm, which is where we found Bernard Koch. He lives right on the edge of the mountain and, on a clear day, they can look over the foothills and see Sydney in the distance. Bernard grows pasture-raised, free-range chickens. The chickens roam all day in a picturesque walnut orchard, pecking at whatever it is that chickens peck at, plus getting a feed of grain as well.

The chickens can stay in the orchard day and night for two very good reasons. First, they're accompanied by Fluffy, a giant Maremma sheep dog. These dogs, originally from Italy, normally bond with a flock of sheep, living with them and protecting them from predators. In this case, Fluffy bonds with the chooks. The second reason they are safe is that Bernard's flock of alpacas lives with the chooks too. These alpacas also have a natural protective instinct. How organic is that!

Way up at Ebenezer in the Blue Mountains there's a remarkable vineyard with an equally remarkable history: Tizzana. So detailed is the architecture that, apart from the gum trees, you'd swear you were in Italy.

Dr Thomas Henry Fiaschi, the builder and namer of Tizzana, was born in Florence, Italy, in 1853. A doctor of medicine, he was also a winemaker. In a speech he gave to the Australian Trained Nurses Association in 1906, he combined his two loves with the words: 'I tell you frankly that I consider the temperate use of a wine a valuable support to the healthy man in this thorny path of life, and that judicious use of it has proved itself to me of incalculable benefit in the treatment of the sick and convalescent.'

At the age of 22 he migrated to Australia and proceeded to build a reputation as an outstanding surgeon. It was this good doctor who introduced Listerian surgery (antiseptic practices where patients and equipment are thoroughly sterilised before surgery) into this country.

As well as consulting honorary surgeon to Sydney Hospital and examiner in clinical surgery at Sydney University, Dr Fiaschi was also president of the NSW Wine Association.

He ended up in the Blue Mountains having decided to move from the city soon after eloping with a nun. In those days that would have created quite a stir. Come to think of it, it would create quite a stir today, too!

At Tizzana they also grow olives and make a robust olive oil.

Back in Sydney we went for an early morning fish on a commercial fishing boat and, on the way back into port, travelled past the Sydney Opera House, under the Harbour Bridge, then on to Sydney's famous Fish Markets where the auction floor was abuzz with bids. The Sydney Fish Market is the largest market of its kind in the southern hemisphere and the world's second largest seafood market in terms of varieties outside of Japan. On any day, more than 100 varieties are up for auction and sale.

Carmelo Aielio, the skipper, showed us to the sashimi room on the auction floor. It was all go, go, go down there. Buyers from all over the world. And the hi-tech Dutch auction system is amazing to watch, too.

Carpaccio of tuna with spanner crab

Tuna and crab — two fantastic ingredients that complement each other. Whenever you serve tuna raw like this, ask your fishmonger for sushi-grade tuna.

SERVES 4

¹/₂ carrot, julienned into 5 cm/2 in lengths
75 g/2 ³/₄ oz celeriac, julienned
into 5 cm/2 in lengths
200 g/7 oz picked crabmeat
1 tablespoon whole egg mayonnaise
8 coriander leaves, finely chopped
sea salt and freshly ground black pepper
2¹/₂ tablespoons extra virgin olive oil
1¹/₂ tablespoons lime juice
1 tablespoon finely chopped chives
400 g/14 oz thick tuna loin, thinly sliced
across the grain
mixed baby herbs, to garnish

1. Bring a small saucepan of water to the boil. Add the carrot and celeriac and cook for 1 minute. Drain and rinse under cold running water. Drain again, then place in a clean tea towel and squeeze out the excess water. Transfer to a bowl, add the crabmeat, mayonnaise, coriander, salt and pepper and mix until combined.

2. Combine the extra virgin olive oil, lime juice and chives in a mixing bowl and pour half of the marinade into a non-metallic flat dish. Add the tuna in a single layer and marinate for 1 minute. Remove the tuna from the dish and arrange on four serving plates.

3. Place a 5 cm/2 in round cutter in the centre of the tuna. Spoon a quarter of the crab mixture into the cutter and smooth the top with the back of a spoon. Gently remove the cutter. Repeat until all the crab mixture is used. Top with baby herbs as garnish.

4. Drizzle the remaining marinade around the outside of the plate and serve.

Curtis Stone

Pan-fried calves' liver with peaches

One of those flavour combinations that surprises. The Italians and the North Africans often do meat and fruit together, with great success. I've seen apricots and duck livers, and quince and liver. Peach and calves' liver gently pan-fried in butter can be described by one word — beautiful.

SERVES 4

100 g/3¹/₂ oz plain flour
sea salt and freshly ground black pepper
4 x 180 g/6¹/₂ oz pieces calves' liver cut into
    slices approximately 1.5 cm/¹/₂ in thick
40 g/1¹/₂ oz butter
2 ripe peaches, each cut into 6 slices
aged balsamic vinegar*, to drizzle
¹/₂ bunch of rocket, trimmed
¹/₄ bunch of mint, leaves picked
shaved parmesan, to serve

1. Season the flour with salt and pepper, and use to dredge the slices of liver. Shake off the excess flour.

2. Melt the butter in a heavy-based frying pan over a medium heat until it starts to foam, add the liver and cook for about 3 minutes or until evenly coloured on each side. Just before the liver is done, add the peach slices and cook until just coloured, but don't overcook.

3. Transfer the liver and peaches to serving plates, season with pepper and drizzle with the balsamic vinegar.

4. Garnish the peach and liver with the rocket, mint and parmesan and serve.

If you don't have aged balsamic vinegar, pour some regular balsamic vinegar into the same pan that the liver and peaches were cooked in and reduce until thick.

Fusilli with mushrooms, olives and ricotta

A quick and easy pasta dish to cook. When we were making the Sydney episode and it was my turn to cook, we only had about five minutes of light left. The cameraman was pulling his hair out, and the director was pulling the cameraman's hair out, so I had to cook fast because neither had much hair to start with! We made it with enough time to eat the whole pot.

SERVES 4

2 tablespoons olive oil

500 g/1 lb 2 oz field mushrooms,
 finely chopped

1 garlic clove, chopped

350 g/12 oz green olives,
 pitted and chopped

250 ml/9 fl oz double/thick cream

1/4 bunch of mint, leaves picked
 and chopped

1/4 bunch of flat leaf parsley,
 leaves picked and chopped

400 g/14 oz fusilli

100 g/3 1/2 oz fresh ricotta, crumbled

100 g/3 1/2 oz parmesan, grated

sea salt and freshly ground black pepper

2 red chillies, chopped

1 lemon, to squeeze

extra virgin olive oil, to drizzle

1. Heat the olive oil in a large heavy-based frying pan over a medium heat and sauté the mushrooms until they release their moisture. Add the garlic and olives and cook until the liquid has evaporated and the flavour is concentrated. Add the cream and simmer until reduced by half. Add half of the mint and parsley, reserving the rest for the garnish.

2. Cook the fusilli until *al dente*, drain and add to the mushroom and olive mixture. Stir in the ricotta and parmesan and season with the salt and pepper. Transfer to warmed pasta bowls and serve garnished with the remaining chopped herbs and the chilli. Drizzle over a squeeze of lemon juice and a little extra virgin olive oil.

Ben O'Donoghue

Fresh pappardelle with confit of duck, pumpkin and sage

Whenever you can, use fresh pasta. It cooks in just 2–4 minutes and is so much nicer than dried pasta.

SERVES 4

3 confit duck legs, meat taken
    off the bone*
1 tablespoon olive oil
300 g/11 oz butternut pumpkin,
    cut into thin wedges
10 freshly ground Szechuan peppercorns
400 g/14 oz fresh pappardelle
100 g/3$\frac{1}{2}$ oz butter
12 sage leaves
juice of 1 orange
1 tablespoon flat leaf parsley, leaves picked
100 g/3$\frac{1}{2}$ oz wild rocket, torn
2$\frac{1}{2}$ tablespoons balsamic vinegar

1. Tear the confit duck leg meat into small chunks.

2. Heat the olive oil in a frying pan over medium heat, add the pumpkin and sauté for 5 minutes or until coloured on one side. Turn and sprinkle with the Szechuan peppercorns.

3. Bring a large pot of salted water to the boil, add the pappardelle and cook until *al dente*. Drain.

4. Add the duck meat to the pumpkin and allow to colour slightly. Add the butter and allow it to turn brown. Add the sage, orange juice, parsley and rocket and mix in the pappardelle until well coated with the sauce.

5. Divide the pappardelle and the sauce between four warmed serving plates, drizzle the balsamic vinegar around the outside of each plate and serve.

* To confit the duck legs, see Rillette of goose with a
chardonnay jelly on page 118 and follow the instructions
for the confit goose legs.

Curtis Stone

Pan-fried blue-eye cod with tomatoes, olives and capers

This simple cod dish is very Mediterranean in style and can be knocked together quite quickly.

SERVES 4

4 new potatoes, peeled

3 tablespoons olive oil

4 x 180 g/6¼ oz blue-eye cod fillets, skin on

sea salt

5 tomatoes, blanched, skinned and cut
    into quarters

4 shallots (eschalots), sliced lengthways

3 teaspoons baby capers (if salted,
    soak in cold water for 30 minutes
    and rinse well)

100 g/3½ oz small, black Niçoise olives

¼ cup finely chopped flat leaf parsley

3 tablespoons lemon juice

3 tablespoons extra virgin olive oil

1. Bring a medium saucepan of salted water to the boil and cook the potatoes until tender. Allow the potatoes to cool, then cut into 5 mm/¼ in slices.

2. Heat 1 tablespoon of the olive oil in a frying pan and cook the potatoes for 1–2 minutes or until golden brown on each side. Drain on paper towel and keep warm.

3. Season both sides of the fish with salt.

4. Heat 1 tablespoon of the remaining olive oil in a frying pan, add the fish and cook, skin-side down, for 2–3 minutes, depending on thickness. Turn over and cook for 1 minute, or until cooked through. Set aside and keep warm.

5. Remove the seeds from the tomatoes and cut into thin strips.

6. Heat the remaining 1 tablespoon of olive oil in a large frying pan and cook the shallots for 1–2 minutes or until softened. Add the tomatoes, capers, olives and parsley and cook, tossing, until just warmed through. Remove from the heat. Stir through the lemon juice and extra virgin olive oil.

7. Arrange the potatoes and a few of the olives in the centre of each serving plate. Spoon the tomato mixture into the middle of the potatoes, place a fish fillet on top and serve.

Curtis Stone

Bender's simple seafood stew

Pair this seafood stew with a fresh baguette.

SERVES 4

2 garlic cloves, chopped
2 pinches of saffron
¹/₂ teaspoon ground ginger
1 teaspoon salt
¹/₄ bunch of coriander roots, finely chopped
¹/₂ bunch of basil, leaves picked
250 ml/9 fl oz water
125 ml/4¹/₂ fl oz white wine
squeeze of lemon juice
4 ripe tomatoes, peeled, deseeded and
   chopped
1 red onion, finely chopped
4 small red mullet, scaled, gutted and
   gills removed
400 g/14 oz selection of firm fish fillets,
   (flathead, leather jacket, scorpion fish,
   cut into chunks)
500 g/1 lb vongole, cleaned
1 kg/2 lb 4 oz mussels, scrubbed and
   debearded
4 oysters, shucked
200 g/7 oz green king prawns, peeled and
   deveined
3 tablespoons olive oil
125 g/4¹/₂ oz canned chickpeas, drained
2 tablespoons roughly chopped flat leaf
   parsley
a good squeeze of lemon juice
sea salt and freshly ground black pepper

1. Pound the garlic, saffron, ginger, salt, coriander roots and half the basil in a mortar. Transfer to a large bowl and add the water, white wine, lemon juice, tomatoes and onion. Stir to combine. Add the seafood and allow to marinate for 10–20 minutes. Chop the remaining basil and set aside.

2. Warm a large, heavy-bottomed pan and add enough olive oil to just cover the bottom. Add the large fish pieces and the marinade. Bring to a simmer and cook, covered, for 10 minutes, turning the fish once or twice.

3. Add the rest of the fish pieces, vongole, mussels, oysters and prawns and cook for 3–5 minutes or until the shellfish are open. Discard any that have not opened. Remove from the heat and stand for 2 minutes. Add the chickpeas, parsley and the remaining basil. Stir in the lemon juice, season to taste with the salt and pepper and serve.

Ben O'Donoghue

Carpaccio of beef with semi-dried tomatoes, confit of garlic and aged goats' cheese

I love carpaccio and I like it with gutsy flavours — and this one has them. Don't over garnish the plate, always have more beef than condiments, and you will get the right balance.

SERVES 4

Confit of garlic

1 large garlic bulb, pulled apart
125 ml/4¹/₂ fl oz olive oil
1 sprig of rosemary

250 g/9 oz cherry tomatoes, blanched
    and peeled
sea salt and freshly ground black pepper
¹/₄ bunch of thyme, leaves picked
    and chopped
250 g/9 oz beef fillet, trimmed of fat
    and sinew
olive oil, for searing
3 teaspoons aged balsamic vinegar
¹/₂ bunch of rocket, trimmed
40 g/1¹/₄ oz aged goats' cheese, shaved,
    to serve
lemon juice, to squeeze

① Preheat the oven to 120°C/250°F/Gas Mark ¹/₂.

② To make the confit of garlic, place the unpeeled garlic cloves in a small saucepan. Add enough olive oil to just cover and add the rosemary. Cook on a very low heat for 20 minutes or until the garlic is soft. Drain on paper towels and reserve the oil.

③ Scatter the cherry tomatoes onto a greaseproof paper-lined oven tray. Sprinkle with salt and pepper and drizzle over a little olive oil from the confit of garlic. Place in the oven and cook for 1 hour until soft and wrinkly and intense in flavour.

④ Sprinkle the thyme onto a plate. Season with salt and pepper and roll over the beef fillet so that it is evenly covered. Heat a heavy-based lightly oiled frying pan over high heat until it gives off a haze. Sear the beef until well browned, approximately 5 minutes, then remove and allow to cool.

⑤ Chop the tomatoes and the garlic flesh. Mix with enough olive oil from the confit of garlic to make a dressing, add the balsamic vinegar and season to taste.

⑥ Slice the beef, then, on a board, smooth the beef flat with the back of a large knife. Arrange on a plate and dress with the tomato and garlic dressing. Garnish with the rocket, goats' cheese and lemon juice.

Roast free-range chicken with truffle butter, carrot puree and watercress

Roast chicken is simply one of the best things in the world — and this one is pretty special. I stole the recipe for the carrot puree from my mate Raymond Capaldi, chef at Fenix in Melbourne, because it's bloody lovely. Thanks, mate!

SERVES 4–6

150 g/5^{1}/$_{2}$ oz butter
10 g/ ^{1}/$_{3}$ oz black truffle, finely chopped
2 garlic cloves, crushed
1 tablespoon finely chopped flat leaf parsley
sea salt and freshly ground black pepper
2 x 1.4 kg/3 lb free-range chickens
1 celery stick, roughly chopped
4 shallots (eschalots), roughly chopped
1 carrot, roughly chopped

Carrot puree
6 carrots, peeled and grated
1 kg/2 lb 4 oz goose fat

2 bunches of watercress, leaves picked

1. Preheat the oven to 200°C/400°F/Gas Mark 6.

2. Combine the butter with the truffle, garlic, parsley, salt and pepper.

3. Beginning from the neck end of the chicken, use your index and middle fingers to push your hand between the skin and meat of both breasts and thighs to create a pocket. Push the butter mixture into the pocket created on each chicken.

4. Scatter the celery, shallots and carrot in a large baking tray and place the chickens on top. Season with salt and pepper and place in the oven for 45–60 minutes. Carefully lift a chicken with a pair of tongs. If the juice runs clear, the chicken is cooked.

5. To make the carrot puree, place the grated carrots in a saucepan and cover with the goose fat. Cook over a very low, almost simmering heat until tender. Strain the carrots from the goose fat, place in a blender and process until smooth. Season with salt and pepper.

6. Serve the carrot puree alongside the chicken and watercress.

Curtis Stone

Beef Wellington

This is my version of the classic English beef dish. I don't like pâté in mine, just loads of English mustard. And I always cook it with the ends open so that the meat jus escapes and the pastry doesn't go soggy.

SERVES 4

1 kg/2 lb 4 oz middle cut beef fillet,
    trimmed
¼ bunch thyme, finely chopped
sea salt and freshly ground black pepper

Duxelles

55 g/2 oz butter
1 clove garlic, finely chopped
500 g/1 lb 2 oz flat field mushrooms,
    finely chopped
few drops of truffle oil
1 tablespoon finely chopped
    flat leaf parsley

English mustard, to taste
500 g/1 lb 2 oz block puff pastry
1 egg, lightly beaten, to seal the pastry

1. Preheat the oven to 180°C/350°F/Gas Mark 4.

2. Season the fillet with the thyme, salt and pepper and allow to rest for 30 minutes so the flavours infuse. Then, in a hot pan, sear each side until golden brown. Allow to cool.

3. To make the duxelles, sweat the butter, garlic and mushrooms in a pan over a low heat until the moisture evaporates. Add the truffle oil and parsley and season with salt and pepper. Allow to cool to room temperature.

4. Smear the cooled fillet with an even coating of English mustard.

5. Lightly dust a sheet of baking paper with flour. Place the block of pastry on top of the baking paper and dust with flour again. Place another sheet of baking paper over the pastry and roll out to a size so that the pastry is a little wider than the fillet and enough so that the fillet can be completely rolled up with 4 cm/1½ in left over.

continued over...

6. Remove the top sheet of baking paper and dust off any excess flour. Place the pastry so the longest half is facing you, and spread the mushroom mixture evenly over the half of pastry closest to you. Place the fillet on top of the mushroom mix.

7. Roll the beef away from you, pulling the pastry firmly around the beef, and leaving 3 cm/1 in of pastry free at the end. Lightly brush this edge with egg and press firmly against the roll so it sticks. Trim the ends of the pastry so they are flush with the beef. Cut a sheet of baking paper to the size of the Beef Wellington and turn the roll so that it rests on the seam on the paper. Lightly brush the top with more egg and put the beef on a baking tray. Refrigerate for 30 minutes.

8. Put the Beef Wellington into the oven and bake for 25 minutes or until the pastry is dark gold in colour. Remove and allow to rest for 10 minutes, then slice with a sharp knife into equal portions.

9. Serve with steamed spinach or your favourite roast vegetables.

Ben O'Donoghue

Terrine of blueberries and sweet wine

Seasonal blueberries have a lovely natural flavour. In this terrine you don't need to cook them so their wonderful taste is retained.

SERVES 6–8

750 ml/1 bottle sweet white wine (botrytis
*   semillon)*
7 leaves of gelatine
4 punnets of blueberries, washed
50 g/2 oz icing sugar, sifted, for dusting
200 ml/7 fl oz cream, lightly whipped

1. Pour the sweet wine into a large saucepan and bring to a simmer.

2. Soak the gelatine in a bowl of cold water until softened. Squeeze out the gelatine leaves and slowly add to the hot wine, stirring constantly.

3. Place the blueberries into a 3½-cup capacity terrine mould. Pour over the wine, reserving 100 ml/3½ fl oz and set in the fridge for 2 hours. (Keep the reserved wine at room temperature so that it doesn't set.)

4. Once the terrine is set, pour the remaining 100 ml/3½ fl oz of wine over the terrine, ensuring that none of the blueberries are above the surface. Return to the fridge for 1 hour.

5. Dip the base of the terrine mould into hot water to loosen the sides. Invert the terrine onto a platter and slice with a warm knife. Dust with the icing sugar and serve with the whipped cream.

Curtis Stone

Mango lassi

There's a little Lahorian restaurant in Whitechapel where I always finish a meal with a lassi, which is basically a yoghurt fruit drink — and it's always great.

SERVES 4

100 g/3 ½ oz ice cubes
750 g/1 lb 10 oz plain yoghurt
200 ml/7 fl oz water
sugar, to taste
2 mangoes, peeled, stone removed and flesh roughly chopped*

1 Put some tall glasses into the refrigerator to chill.

2 Crush the ice in a blender.

3 Add the yoghurt, water, sugar and mango and blend until smooth.

4 Pour into the chilled glasses and serve.

*Note: You can substitute the mango with other fruit or flavours.

Ben O'Donoghue

Acknowledgements

Ben O'Donoghue

I can't say how happy and excited I was at being able to do another series of *Surfing the Menu* and book to go with it. I had so much fun the first time around and made some brilliant friends, so I would like to thank God, Marian Bartsch and Richard Reisz for this wonderful opportunity, and also the ABC for having some faith in the show and the people involved in it.

To my wife the lovely De-arne Wicks (yes, she has kept her name and I'm cool with that) thank you for loving me, supporting me and kicking my butt when needed, and thank you for being the best mum in the world to our Ruby.

To Stonie: you're the man, you're a champion, and I learnt a lot from our time together. You're surfing is still rubbish but you're a damn fine chef. (so here's one for the good guys!).

To all the crew involved in the show: Alun Bartsch, Paul Bell, Lozza, Graigie, Herps, Ulli, Kelvinator, Ursie, Sarah Shaw, Matteo, and the talented director Simon Target (as in the store), and the editor Beckett Broad, who has watched more of me and Curtis than anyone could possibly want to. You're all so amazing, you're like family and with luck we'll work together again some day soon.

And thank you to all the amazing people we met on the way round: Boomer, Tash and the boys, Gerry the sick man who likes near death experiences, and Luke – thanks and I hope we meet again.

To Susan Morris-Yates, the calmest, most patient editor in the world, thank you.

Thanks, of course, to Martine and Michelle at DML for just doing what they do best and that is to hassle me for recipes. I love to you both.

I would like to dedicate my part of the book to the loving memory of my grandma, Dorothy Harpley.

Curtis Stone

After the first series of *Surfing the Menu* I felt very lucky to have worked with such an amazing crew. So it was brilliant to have more or less the same crew the second time around. And while we missed Jeff and Kerry very much, it was also great to work with Simon Target, the new director. Simon, thank God, is a real foodie with as much passion for food as for telling a story.

The crew, headed by Marian and Alun Bartch, is more like a family than a group of people working together. Over the eight-week shoot we got to meet Ulli the DOP's two lovely little girls; Laurie the sound technician's wife and their two little girls; and Simon's wife and two boys, cool dudes even if Bender did throw one of them off the Rottenest pier fully dressed. As everybody's families and girlfriends would drop in and enjoy the scenery and good food they would also lend a hand, to help make the show what it is.

To my amazement, Kelvin the line producer always had us on time and always had a smile on his face. The location photography is spectacular. At times we were hanging out of a chopper or off the side of a boat, so Craig and Ewan thanks for the great shoots.

Anyone who knows me will say that I am fairly laid back unless, of course, they have worked with me in a kitchen. There I am a pedantic and particular bastard, always wanting the best and the freshest. The problem is that when you are traveling around obscure parts of Australia, finding the freshest is not always quite that easy. So a special thanks to Ursula the home economist for going the extra yard – and on occasion producing miracles.

Food photography in a book is never easy when there is limited time, so Christine Shepard, the home economist, and food stylist Michelle Noerianto have done an amazing job. It was great to have an ex-chef, Steve Brown, do the photography. Thanks for giving me the freedom and support.

During the twelve months I was back in Australia, I cooked a few times in restaurants. I was lucky enough to have the support of two of the best chefs and their brigades in the country: Shannon Bennett from Vue De Monde in Melbourne and Matt Moran from Aria in Sydney.

Big thanks to Martine Carter (my agent, and Bender's) for all of your tireless work. You must be regretting the day you signed us both on as clients. Also a special thanks to Karzi (my chief recipe taster) for all your help and support. Of course I have to mention my amazing family: Lozza and Golly, Dad and Sue, my brother, and all of my great mates who are always there for me.

And Bender, what can I say? You are a bloody legend.

Index

Conversion chart

75 mL	2½ fl oz	15 g	½ oz
100 mL	3½ fl oz	30 g	1 oz
125 mL	4½ fl oz	55 g	2 oz
150 mL	5½ fl oz	75 g	2¾ oz
200 mL	7 fl oz	100 g	3½ oz
250 mL	9 fl oz	125 g	4½ oz
300 mL	10½ fl oz	150 g	5½ oz
450 mL	¾ pt	200 g	7 oz
500 mL	18 fl oz	225 g	8 oz
600 mL	1 pt	250 g	9 oz
800 mL	1½ pt	300 g	11 oz
1 L	1¾ pt	350 g	12 oz
1.2 L	2 pt	400 g	14 oz
1.5 L	2⅔ pt	450 g	1 lb
2 L	3½ pt	500 g	1 lb 2 oz
2.5 L	4½ pt	700 g	1½ lb
4 L	7 pt	900 g	2 lb
		1 kg	2 lb 4 oz
		1.2 kg	¾ lb
		1.4 kg	3 lb
		1.5 kg	3 lb 5 oz
		2 kg	4½ lb
		5 kg	11 lb